Broken
BEFORE
GOD

when faith and
calamity collide

Brandt
Johnson

Broken Before God: When Faith and Calamity Collide
© 2024 Brandt Johnson

If you have questions or would like to arrange speaking engagements, please contact the author at bcjohnsonbooks@gmail.com

ISBN (paperback): 979-89908796-9-0
ISBN (eBook): 979-89908796-8-3
ISBN (Hardcover): 979-89908796-7-6
ISBN (audiobook): 979-89908796-6-9

Published by: capital theta

Edited by: Ron Broach

Cover Art: Mac McEndree

Dedication

To my amazing wife, Jennifer:
You have stuck by my side
through ups, downs, ins, outs,
backs, and forths. You showed me what
God's love really looks like.
You helped me understand
faithfulness through your example.
You have loved me
despite my brokenness.
I love you.

Acknowledgment

Special thanks to my father, Dennis Johnson, for challenging me to "write it down." I would have never completed this if it was not for you.

Thanks Dad!

Preface

Again I saw that under the sun
the race is not to the swift,
nor the battle to the strong,
nor bread to the wise,
nor riches to the intelligent,
nor favor to those with knowledge,
but time and chance happen to them all.

Ecclesiastes 9:11 (ESV)

I know there are many ideas out there as to how God operates. Does he cause things to happen or just allow them? I am not trying to debate any of these ideas with this book. However, before I get too far, I want to establish a few points. These points reflect my interpretation and are not hard-and-fast rules everyone must hold. If you do not believe the same as I do, that is ok. I simply want you to understand my perspective as I share the following experiences. You may not agree with any of these points, but it will help you understand my perspective as I faced the situations you will read about in the following pages.

I believe God is in control—a sovereign God—and he knows our every choice and movement. However, I do not believe we are mere chess pieces that God is moving around on a cosmic chessboard. I believe God calls some people with specific tasks. I do not believe every individual has a specific path they must find to be within "God's will," and if you make the wrong choice, you are outside of it. I believe God knows what is best for us, and although we often think we know what is best, we are often wrong. I believe that, in knowing our every step, God is not necessarily dictating our every step. I believe in a God who interacts with his creation, and this interaction is often a response to prayers. I believe God has laid out a specific plan for everyone, and some things happen as a direct intervention from God. But in a broad sense (i.e. Christ's death, burial, and resurrection), I do not believe everything "happens for a reason."

For example, let's consider Moses and Samuel. These individuals had direct callings. God specifically called or directed them to distinct paths for their lives. But what about Uzzah, Paltiel, or Eutychus? Uzzah simply reached out his hand to steady the Ark of the Covenant while it was being transported on a cart and was struck dead. Paltiel married Michal, King Saul's daughter, after David (who married Michal after paying 100 Philistine foreskins to King Saul) was run out of the kingdom. Paltiel then had to give Michal up when David wanted her back. Eutychus was tired, went to sleep, and fell out a window. Some would argue these were all predestined incidents that took place specifically by God's design. I would note God's design is referenced in stories like the man born blind "that the works of God might be displayed in him" (John 9:3 NIV). The other narratives in scripture above are just that—narrative—an account that it happened.

I was nineteen years old and decided I needed a change in my life. I had moved back in with my parents the year before and was looking for direction. I had three opportunities to choose from. I was praying for God's direction and that He would show me His "will." When I heard nothing, I asked my dad for advice. He asked me if I would be able to serve both God and others in each of the places I was considering. After consideration, I told him I could do those things anywhere I go. He said, "Then it sounds like it is up to you."

Admittedly, I have felt God calling me specifically in certain situations of my life, but it is not every event in every moment of every day. Some things just happen, and that is ok. Sometimes things may be considered good, and other times they may be considered bad. Whether they are good or bad, some things just happen.

As quoted above, Ecclesiastes 9:11 says some things happen as a result of time and chance. This does not diminish the sovereignty of God or detract from the call to accomplish his work. Sometimes God calls people to accomplish very specific tasks. His Spirit is absolutely at work in our lives to guide us into works that will further His kingdom. Accidents are also a possibility. These accidents can alter our lives. When we face these situations, we can despair and turn away from God; remain neutral and do nothing; or use the circumstances to glorify God. The choice is yours. It is up to you to decide to give God the glory in whatever situation you find yourself.

I am an American and a Christian. The following content is founded within this framework. The context around each chapter will often be explained, but the overarching circumstances are limited to my perspective. Your understanding, dear reader, of this context will often be assumed. I know not everyone is American, nor is everyone reading this Christian. However, those two markers will define the entirety of the following.

Each chapter will include some narrative of the events surrounding my motorcycle accident. At the end of each chapter, I will include some considerations relevant to the situation. These considerations will include thoughts, expressions, or ideals peculiar to being an American and a Christian. Bible passages, doctrinal teachings, and even personal beliefs or standards will be included in these interjections. These are my opinions or ideas that were developed as a result of my experience. Please understand, I am on a journey through this life, just like the rest of us, and I am still trying to figure this whole thing out.

I will state some things as empirical, though they may only seem so in my understanding. For instance, as I stated above, I believe God is sovereign. This I hold, not based on a Bible verse or a doctrinal teaching, but from personal experience. If you are inclined to disagree with me on any of these points, I understand, and I am ok with that. I may read this a year from now and discover I too disagree. But that is why life is considered a journey; there is always something new to discover. I am only writing about what I have experienced and discovered so far. I still have a lot to learn!

You will hear some negative tones relative to my upbringing or the teaching I heard as a young person. I want to clarify from the beginning of this book that I had very Godly parents. They were the best depiction I had of what it meant to be followers of Jesus. The references to teachings that caused angst—and sometimes outright rebellion—were teachings from the church in which I was raised. These may not have been direct teachings from the pulpit or exact doctrines from a teacher, but they were mostly what I gleaned from observation of the lifestyles of those who were teaching. The words they taught were one thing, but the way they treated people was totally different. My issues were not with my parents, but with the inconsistencies between what people stated as truth and what they lived. Their actions did not match their words. Regardless of the context, this situation will inevitably lead to confusion.

Please use these preceding words, not as law, but as a filter through which you read the following story. God is in control, but this does not mean we are puppets. Bad things can happen by chance, but that does not mean we are victims. Our goal in life is to glorify God in our actions and words, and to serve others in ways we would want to be served. I hope this helps as you read through my journey that follows.

Introduction

Why do bad things happen to good people? This question has often been answered with over-spiritualized melodrama. Other times the answer is shrouded in arcane technical Christianese that doesn't satisfy the questioner. Recently I came up with a satisfying answer, and it makes a lot of sense to me. During a discussion with a Christian peer who was explaining how this question had been posed to him, I simply replied, "I don't know," and, after a momentary pause, added, "but I am ok with that."

You see, faith in God and believing He is in control even when bad things happen allows us to have peace that, as Philippians 4:7 tells us, goes beyond understanding. We do not have to understand the causation, explanation, or spiritual lesson demanded by every "bad" event. That being said, wisdom can help us navigate these circumstances. Encouragement from others can help us bear the weight of them. A strong faith that God is in control can motivate us to push forward even though we might be in the middle of the "valley of the shadow of death."

Speaking of the valley from Psalm 23, did you know the same author also wrote this, "You [God] have thrown me into the lowest pit, into the darkest depths...You have driven my friends away by making me repulsive to them. I am in a trap with no way of escape." —Psalm 88:6a, 8 (NLT).

How does this same person, who feels God betrayed him and caused all kinds of bad things to happen, also affirm God's comfort, peace, and steadfastness? I believe it is because this author had peace that goes beyond understanding. He did not have to know why the bad things were happening or the spiritual meaning behind every situation. He simply laid everything at the feet of his Lord.

I believe this same principle applies to the question about why bad things happen. We do not have to know the answer, nor do we need to explain it away in order to have peace. And sometimes, we will even feel abandoned, outcast, or hopeless. But the grounding factor is the peace you can feel when you know you are not the one in control of everything. You are not the sovereign one. And, even though we may never get the answer to our question, "why?" we can be ok with it.

Paul, the author of the letter to the Philippians, described what it is like to experience both abundance and poverty. That is when he lays out the iconic phrase, "...I have learned, in whatsoever state I am, therewith to be content." —Philippians 4:11b (KJV). This is not a roll-over-and-be-a-doormat attitude. It is simply knowing who is in control and is actually sitting on the throne. Boy am I glad it is not me!

Jesus demonstrated this same attitude when he was being jeered and tormented. 1 Peter 2 clues us in when the author writes, "When they hurled their insults at him, he did not retaliate; when he suffered, he made no threats. Instead, he entrusted himself to him who judges justly."(NIV). He knew these people who were hurting him were not the ones he would be answerable to. Our judge is God alone!

On the following pages, you will read a first-person account of my near-fatal motorcycle accident. You will see not only my physical struggles, but my spiritual struggles as well. Most of what you will read are things I tried to work through for many years prior to this accident. You will also see new struggles arise as a result. And, of course, you will see several instances where the lightbulb finally clicks on regarding many of the things I have wrestled with throughout my life.

Even though I was raised in the church, went to a Bible college, memorized a ton of scripture, and served as a pastor for several years, I never truly grasped the full meaning of God and his gospel message. There were ideas and theologies I had twisted and warped in my mind. This is the story of how I became broken before my God. Yes, in a literal sense, as well as metaphorical.

My body was broken, and I was helpless to do anything about it on my own. And inside my body, my heart was broken and laid helpless before my creator. You will read about my bodily pains and my spiritual pains. You will also read about healing for both.

Each chapter begins with a physical account, followed by spiritual lessons—things that came to mind during my physical pains, struggles, and healings. The first part of each chapter is my story, but it could be anyone's story. We have all faced trouble in one way or another. Pain is pain, whether resulting from a motorcycle accident, the death of a loved one, childhood trauma, a cancer diagnosis, or abuse. The list could go on. However, God's grace is sufficient no matter what has caused the pain in your life.

I wrote this book, not just to share my story, but to share how God brought me through my story and to encourage you in your story. Each one of us has unique experiences that take us down different roads, but the God of Heaven and Earth is right there with us through our journey. This book is so much more about the lessons I learned than it is about the narrative that led me to those lessons.

I know without a doubt God used my situation to grab my attention and call me into a deeper relationship with him. And, just as he did with me, he wants to do this with you as well. I pray you can listen to my story and come to experience this deeper life with God without going through what I had to go through.

I have much more progress to make, but the next steps will be a lot closer to God than the ones behind me. In this life we will face struggles. Here is an account of my journey so far.

Contents

The Accident 1

The Aftermath 7

The Injuries 13

The Hospital 21

My Darkest Night 27

Rehab 35

The Realization 43

The Struggle 51

The Body 61

Broken 69

Faithfulness 77

Afterward 85

The Accident

Four wheels move the body;
Two wheels move the soul.
—Author Unknown

The date was June 30, 2023. It was approximately 4:15 p.m. The temperature was 81° (F), and the wind was out of the NW at 11mph. Ok, I actually had to look that information up, but I do remember it was hot.

I was just finishing work for the day. I had started a new work-from-home job about two months earlier. My wife, Jennifer, worked on the opposite side of town where a lot of businesses were located in our growing rural town. I had arranged to meet her at a store after work for some errands. This was not a common occurrence, at least not lately. Some days, if we had errands, Jennifer would drive home, pick me up, and then drive back into town. More often, she would complete the errands without me on her way home. But this was a special occasion to pick up a surprise gift for her. Little did I know just how big of a surprise the day would bring.

I had recently sold my truck because I was now working from home and I rarely drove it anymore. There was a two-week period where I never even started the thing. That's when I decided it was not worth the payments to be sitting there in the driveway. I did have transportation though, a 1997 Honda Shadow VLX 600. It was yellow and black and a joy to ride! I learned how to drive a motorcycle on my father's Honda

Shadow when I was sixteen years old. A few years after my wife and I were married, I had purchased a different Honda Shadow from my dad.

Needless to say, I enjoyed riding motorcycles. I had taught my sister and my wife to ride. I was not a professional rider by any stretch of the imagination, but I was responsible and confident in my skills. I had only laid my bike down once in my entire life, and that was only a few weeks after I learned how to ride. I was in a gravel parking lot—if you know, you know. Gravel and motorcycles do not play well together. I wasn't hurt, but more importantly, my dad's bike wasn't hurt (he may be hearing about this for the first time right now...Sorry, Dad!).

Other than that minor spill in the parking lot, I never again felt out-of-place riding a bike. I felt like Bob Seger trying to decide if I should go east or west! I loved riding. The roar of the bike, the rush of the wind, and the freedom of the open road! There will always be a spot in my heart for that feeling.

This particular day, I walked to the bike as I had countless times before. In the state where I live, there are no laws requiring motorcyclists to wear helmets. The only protective equipment required by law is eye protection. I typically would at least wear my leather jacket, which is equipped with a full skid-plate in the back. But, didn't I mention, it was hot! I put on my sunglasses and, like Bob Seger himself, just rolled that power on.

Since my family and I like to avoid town and traffic as much as possible, we live a few miles outside of town. On our rural road, it was peaceful and quiet that fateful day. I turned off our dirt road and onto the main road to town, and there was not a soul in sight.

I won't go into the details of our errands, but, to put it plainly, I was excited. I was looking at a gift for my wife and, as I said earlier, it was a surprise. I rarely pull off surprises when it comes to gifts for her, so this was one of those rare occasions where it looked like it was actually going to work.

I am often in my own head while I am driving a four-wheeled vehicle, but when I am only on two wheels, I have to be a lot more defensive. I am scanning the road ahead and behind in my mirrors while I am on a motorcycle. This day was no different. Even with all the excitement going on between my ears, I was focused on the road.

Up ahead, I saw a black SUV pulled to the opposite side of the road, facing me. On this particular road, everyone's mailboxes are on the same side of the road. The vehicle facing me was off the shoulder on my side of the road, but he was facing me. My eyes fed my brain the information—this guy was checking his mail. No problem. Everyone did it. He was on his way home, pulled across traffic to check his mailbox on the opposite side of the road from his driveway. This happens all the time, so I simply shifted further over toward the center line to give me plenty of room and stay visible to any oncoming traffic.

My eyes continued scanning. Further up the road, a half-mile, maybe less, a law enforcement vehicle was pulled over on the same side of the road with his lights spinning. I instinctively did what everyone else does when they see red and blue lights flashing; I checked my speedometer. I was going the speed limit—safe, right?

No, not safe. The black SUV started pulling away from his mailbox and into my path. I had already moved toward the center of the road, so swerving was kind-of out of the question. So all I had time to do was hit my breaks—hard. The rear brake locked up and I could hear the screech of the tires. For approximately four seconds, an exaggeratedly long four seconds, I rushed toward the side of the SUV at 55mph.

Several days later, my wife stopped by the scene and measured the skid marks. I had skidded for sixty-eight feet before I struck the other vehicle!

People ask me if I ever lost conciseness or blacked out. They ask what went through my mind. Honestly, I remember thinking, "Well, this is it...And that's ok."

Lesson Learned

"There are no accidents."
—Grand Master Oogway, Kung Fu Panda

The above quote seems to be mostly philosophical, but bear in mind: Oogway is a fictitious character from a cartoon.

There is also a popular quote from Bob Ross. "There are no mistakes, only happy accidents."

You would be surprised at how many quotes there are regarding accidents and their nature. I read through a lot of them while researching this chapter. Interesting fact: there are about as many views of accidents as there are accidents! Some insist everything is predestined and how a frustrating delay in their routine caused them to avoid a car wreck. What about the people who were in the wreck? Why would you think the universe, or higher power, or karma, likes you better than them? You see, it is easy for us to keep our focus on ourselves and our own situations and pay no heed to the rest of the world.

We live as if the world revolves around the story of our lives. We think everyone else is a supporting actor or an extra, or even an expendable crew member. It is our nature to think this way. It is normal to be self-centered. That is what made Christ-followers so aberrant. They were self-less. They gave of themselves for the sake of others, as Christ taught. Paul, one of the Apostles, even said we need to think of others as "more important than yourselves" —Phil. 2:3 (NASB).

What does this have to do with accidents? Well, after my accident, it would have been very easy to stay focused on myself, my pain, my discomfort, or any number of selfish things. But, through this one event, my eyes were opened to the people around me who were sucked into my drama—or was I sucked into theirs?

There was my family, who was greatly impacted by the accident. The other driver was impacted (quite literally I might add). There were people who stopped to help. The ambulance drivers. The officer who responded to the scene, the helicopter pilot, the nurses, doctors, and EMTs who worked on me, the surgeons, my extended family, my church family all across the world! There were literally thousands of people who had some kind of impact from this one event! Yes, it was my accident, but so many people were either forced or chose to be involved as a result of the accident.

I was not the central player. I should never think I am the central player. If Christ is not the central player, then my focus is off. Through my accident, I saw the futility of trying to be the central focus in a world where everyone else wants the same thing. I could easily have become a legend in my own mind as I focused on myself and all the things that would change for me. But, instead, it was amazing to see how many people I was able to interact with because I was in this accident.

Chapter 1 - The Accident

The thoughtful reader may interject here, "Ah, see there *was* a purpose for your accident. It was so you could interact with all those people." You may very well be right, or was the purpose so they could interact with me? Either way, this incident forced us to interact, even if the only thing I learned was recognizing that if every individual is the main player then no one is the main player. If it was just understanding the futility of this, then that was enough. But, as you will read in the next chapters, there were so many more lessons to learn.

As I write this now, I am reminded of a scripture, "...creation was subject to futility, not willingly, but because of him who subjected it, in hope that the creation itself will be set free from its bondage to corruption and obtain the freedom of the glory of the children of God." —Romans 8:20, 21 (NASB). This forces me to think of the reality of being free in Christ. Not freedom from sin, or hurt, or even death, but freedom from self. In this life we can become slaves trapped inside our own mind, bound to ourself, or at least our self-image. This is a kind of idol worship. It is a way we create a god in our own image. This made me realize I can become so focused on taking care of myself that it turns to self-centeredness.

Don't get me wrong, we need to take care of ourselves. I will speak to that end later, because, believe me, there was a lot of self-care needed after my accident. But we do not have to be trapped in self care. I have experienced this trap. I got so wrapped up in my own mind I did not even realize how it was affecting the people around me—people who loved me and cared for me.

Our actions have reactions. Our choices will have after-effects. Sometimes the actions we produce may be innocent, or even accidental. I certainly did not set out that day intending to run into the side of someone's vehicle. But it happened. However you view it—whether by accident or by design—it happened. One thing I learned from this experience was: *You should not focus on the accident, instead, focus on how you respond to it.* People will see your true character when they witness what you do next.

In Luke 6, Jesus told his disciples, "...a tree is known by its fruit." He was demonstrating that you can tell what kind of person someone is by the actions you see in their lives. In verse 45, he says, "The good person out of the good treasure of his heart produces good, and the evil person out of his evil treasure produces evil, for out of the abundance of the heart his mouth speaks." (ESV)

What you have built up in your heart is going to come out when you face adversity. In this life we will have trouble! How you respond to it will show your true character to those around you.

The Aftermath

"You, me, or nobody, is gonna hit as hard as life, but it ain't about how hard you hit, it's about how hard you can get hit and keep moving forward..."

—Sylvester Stallone as Rocky Balboa
Rocky (1976)

My eyes were wide open, the sound of screeching tires filled my ears, and then, impact. I saw and felt nothing for a split second. I actually don't remember landing on the ground. There was just pain—immense pain. Then I called out to whoever would listen, "Help, help, I am hurt! Help!"

I was lying on my back with my knees up and feet flat on the ground. There was a combination of burning and stabbing pain radiating from my hips and lower back. It was the worst pain I had ever felt up to that point. I had no idea what kind of shape I would find my body when I opened my eyes. I kept them closed for the moment and focused on the pain.

You know those pain charts they have in hospitals and clinics? I have always been terrible at those. Admittedly, I am overly analytical. I had never felt the worst pain in my life, so how would I choose a pain level as it compared to that amount of pain? Well, I suddenly had a reference point!

I moved my arms around. Flexed my wrists and ankles. I even picked my head up and finally opened my eyes to glance around. Laying my head on the ground I thought, "I'm fine. I'm not paralyzed. I just need to stop this pain!" Somehow I had the sense to just lie still. And I *really* had to use a restroom!

I have no concept of how much time passed before someone arrived. Remember the officer I saw further down the road? It was him. I found out later the officer had pulled over to retrieve a tire from the middle of the road when the accident happened. Now he was kneeling beside me, assessing the situation. He asked all the typical questions and told me to lie still.

I was hot. After all, I was lying flat on my back, on the pavement, on an eighty-degree day! I was parched and covered in sweat. Someone else was there too. This Good Samaritan brought me something to put under my head so it wasn't resting on the ground. And he gave me a bottle of water! It is not easy to drink while lying down, but I managed, and it was such a relief.

I suddenly remembered I was on my way to meet my wife. I fished my phone out of my pocket and called her to let her know I was ok, but I was in an accident. I explained an ambulance was on its way and they were taking me to the hospital. I told her I thought I was fine; there was no blood, and everything seemed to be working. She was still at work and told me she would just meet me at the hospital when she was done with work.

I then handed my phone to the Good Samaritan and asked him to take a picture just to show Jennifer I was all in one piece. I had him take a picture of the bike too. He handed my phone back and I texted the photos to her.

In the meantime, I was getting antsy lying there as the pain increased. I asked if someone would help me straighten my legs because my hips were hurting. In reality I wanted them to help me up so I could just walk it off! In my mind this was all much ado about nothing! But I was told to just lie still and not move. I tried to assure the naysayers I was fine. And I truly believed I was. I imagined our trip to camp would be delayed because of the annoying hospital visit, but we would eventually get on the road—we'd just be a little late.

The ambulance finally arrived. It had taken about forty-five minutes to cross town. I found out later it was delayed because they were debating on whether or not to send a helicopter to pick me up on the side of the road. Alas, they sent the ambulance. The ambulance pulled to the side of the road and the paramedics jumped out. Then things started getting pretty complicated. The ambulance crew started working quickly. They got a support belt under me and pinched it tightly around my pelvic region. This was excruciating and the pain shot through my entire body like a prolonged electric shock as they cinched the brace tighter. The brace was an attempt to close the pelvic fracture they assumed after their quick triage. It would also slow any internal bleeding which they determined was highly probable. I found out later this simple procedure probably saved my life.

The shock was now wearing off and I realized how much pain I was in. Of course, I had hardly moved since the accident and now I was being poked and prodded and asked a ton of questions. I never lost consciousness, but most of the next several minutes were a bit fuzzy. I remember being rolled over so they could put the support belt on me and rolled again to be put onto some kind of hammock thing they used to lift me onto the gurney. There was so much pain now I mostly just closed my eyes and clenched my jaw in between cries of pain.

Once I was secured on the gurney, they lifted me into the back of the ambulance. I caught a glimpse of the traffic that had accumulated around me, but it was too blurry to relay anything with much details. The two emergency workers were talking fast now and their voices seemed to me to be at a far distance — but I could hear them and understand. One of them was attempting to get an IV started while the other was cutting my clothes off with scissors. Somewhere in this clamor they had given me some medication for the pain.

I found out later that the EMTs could not get the IV going because my blood pressure was too low. They were right about the pelvic fracture, which had caused heavy internal bleeding. This became my biggest problem over the next several hours. The EMTs made the call that I would need to be airlifted to the closest Level I Trauma Center. All my life I have wanted to ride in a helicopter and now I would get my wish.

Lesson Learned

"Trust in the Lord with all your heart,
and do not lean on your own understanding.
In all your ways acknowledge him,
and he will make straight your paths."
—Proverbs 3:5,6 (ESV)

I would love to tell you I was constantly in prayer and focused on God during this whole incident, but I wasn't. I was focusing mostly on the pain and the fact that my plans fell through. I was thinking about missing out on picking up my wife's gift. I was thinking about how we should just clear this up and give me something for the pain so I could be released from the hospital. We needed to get on the road if we were going to make it up to the camp. I had no idea what I was in for.

Our plans often do not go the way we want them to. Do we take the time to acknowledge the Lord in those times? It wasn't until several days later that this verse actually popped into my head. It made me think about a sermon series I had preached on Jonah.

Here is a great example of God directly calling someone to a specific task. God tells Jonah to go to Nineveh to proclaim God's judgment over the city. Jonah doesn't want to do this and gets on a boat in the opposite direction. A huge storm comes up and Jonah tells the crew to throw him into the water and that will calm the storm. That was always crazy to me, this guy would rather die than to do what God was calling him to do!

Jonah 1:17-2:1 says, "...The LORD appointed a great fish to swallow up Jonah. And Jonah was in the belly of the fish for three days and three nights. Then Jonah prayed to the LORD his God from the belly of the fish." (ESV)

Why did it take three days for Jonah to decide to call out to God? Of course we can only speculate, but, in my mind I picture Jonah trying with all his might to figure out how to get out of this horrible situation! That is typical human behavior. We find ourselves in a bind. We work and work on trying to figure out how to get out of the mess. I imagine Jonah doing the same thing. Then after exhausting all of his efforts, he resigns himself to call out to God.

I believe in a God who interacts with his creation, and this is often his response to our prayers. He wants to interact with us but we have the free will to ignore him. We can choose not to call out to God, and sometimes the period of time where we are trying to solve our own problems lasts a lot longer than three days! This made me think of all the times I struggled through tough situations without ever thinking to call out to God.

Now keep in mind, just because we call out to God does not mean he will simply remove our troubles, fix our problems, and relieve all our pain. He can do all those things, and sometimes he does. But not always. God does not always answer prayers the way we want based solely on the fact that we are good people who believe in him.

Prayer is not an incantation that works if we do it right and doesn't work if we do it wrong. I have found that in prayer we should be less focused on the posture of our body—hands folded, head bowed, eyes closed—than the posture of our heart. We can always bring requests to God, even do so boldly, but our request does not mean God is then obligated to answer with a "yes."

God is not a holy butler who exists to give us our every wish or desire. He looks into our heart and finds the motivation behind our desire. He knows why we want the things we ask for. It seems this is what happened to Jonah. Even after finally calling out to God he still ended up having to go to Nineveh. God did not save him from the fish and send him back to the comforts of his own home. Rather God sent him to continue his original mission.

I cannot give you a formula of how to get God to answer the way you want him to. But I can tell you how foolish I would be to assume that I can manipulate God. Even though I often try, It just doesn't work. For me, it often goes like this: I find myself in some sort of bad situation, probably as a result of some terrible choice I made. But, in all of my wisdom, I will devise the best solution to my problem. Then, once I attempt to accomplish that solution and fail numerous times, I finally call out to God. "Hey, I am in this tight spot here, but don't worry, I already figured out the answer. All I need you to do is..." Then when God doesn't come through on his end of the bargain, I get mad at God. Sounds foolish, right?

God wants to be acknowledged. He wants us to be able to turn to him and fully rely on him whether or not things go the way we want them to. If we rely on God when things are going well in our lives, but turn away from him when things don't go our way, we are nothing but spoiled brats.

I had some very specific plans that day when I headed into town. I knew the results of my plans. I had communicated those plans with others around me. The best laid schemes of mice and men, right?

Let's look at it in a slightly different light. James 4 mentions boasting about our plans for the future and gives this as a kind of warning, "Instead you ought to say, 'If the Lord wills, we shall live and do this or that.'" (NKJV). This is not prescriptive or algorithmic, meaning that as long as you qualify your plans with this phrase then you are good to go. It is not simply a cop-out giving you an excuse if you fail at something to blame it on not being 'within the Lord's will.' It is an acknowledgment of God. It is knowing our place before him. It is an admittance that he is God and I am not!

Proverbs 3:5, as we saw above, states, "...we should not lean on our own understanding..." It admonishes us to trust in the Lord and recognize that he is present in every situation. We can be sure he will walk with us through the good times and the bad times! We can trust God will never leave us nor will he forsake us. Whether we are on top of the world or in the belly of a fish, God is with us. Even when we don't 'feel' his presence, we can know he is there.

Just remember how often we end up in bad situations because of our foolish choices. Rather than blame God, we can acknowledge that he is there. It did take me several days before I recognized I was in pretty rough shape. The true reality of how close I actually was to dying wouldn't come for about another month. I have always been a little slow on the uptake, if you know what I mean. But, I eventually got to the point of acknowledging God. It didn't make everything better, or remove all of my pain, or instantly heal my broken body. But it did allow me to revel in the fact that an all-powerful sovereign God was right beside me every step of the way.

The Injuries

Broken does not mean
non-functioning, or incapacitated,
it does however mean
ready for repair.
—Shawn Boreta

An open-book pelvic fracture is exactly what it sounds like. The impact from the handlebars of the motorcycle hit my hip bones with so much force that my hips folded back like an open book. There is a joint where the two iliac (hip) bones come together in the front, called the pubic symphysis. About four inches separated this joint, which doesn't move much in a typical situation. The pressure also caused a fracture in my sacrum, which is the next bone up from the tailbone, where the hip and spine connect.

In the last chapter, I said the open-book pelvic fracture became my biggest problem because of the internal bleeding. However, the sacral fracture was a significant issue as well. The sacrum is home to a large portion of the nerves coming off the base of the spine (I do not know all the medical terminologies, so please accept my layman's view). If these nerves received too much damage, I could have lost a lot more than a couple pints of blood, including control over bodily functions or even my ability to walk.

Along with the "structural" damage suffered, there was a large amount of soft-tissue damage, tearing connective ligaments, and massive bruising. The full extent of this type of damage was never fully explored. Mostly because very little can be done from a medical perspective — other than let the natural process of my body take over to re-grow and heal the ruined tissue.

On the outside of my body, you could hardly tell I was in an accident. There was no blood, twisted limbs, or disfigured features. I had a half-inch cut on my right elbow, three parallel scrapes on my left thigh about three inches long, and a tiny scratch on my forehead—probably from my sunglasses, which were not even broken.

Lesson Learned

**What sorrow awaits you
teachers of religious law
and you Pharisees. Hypocrites!
For you are so careful to clean the
outside of the cup and the dish,
but inside you are filthy—
full of greed and self-indulgence!
—Matthew 23:25 (NLT)**

One trend I see in the accounts of Jesus's life is that he was often harsh when dealing with the religious leaders and Pharisees. He called them out on their legalism and hypocrisy. Shortly after the verse above, Jesus called them 'white-washed tombs' because they looked all nice and clean on the outside, but they were filled with the bones of dead people. "Outwardly you look like righteous people, but inwardly your hearts are filled with hypocrisy and lawlessness." —Matthew 23:28 (NLT).

For many years I never even thought this verse could be applied to me. I just knew Christians should not act like the Pharisees, the religious leaders, and the teachers of the law. Those guys were hypocrites! And I knew hypocrites were bad. Since I am not a Pharisee—one of the bad-guys—I can probably just skip these verses.

I figured any verse where Jesus was calling out the religious leaders was certainly only meant for sinners! Jesus had problems with these groups and he was not afraid to point out their faults. I, obviously, don't have any faults. Being a good person has always been important to me. I had studied the scriptures enough to know I was spot-on in all my doctrinal beliefs. I was the epitome of what it meant to be godly. I was...holy moly, I was a Pharisee! I was a hypocrite!

So, what *is* a hypocrite? I think we often get this one wrong. I think our understanding of hypocrisy is often misleading or even deflecting a harsh reality. Let me explain. We all have heard expressions of reluctance toward church attendance based on the excuse that the church is full of hypocrites! A common reaction I have heard is, "Good!" As if the church being filled with hypocrisy is a good and acceptable thing.

Now, don't get me wrong, hypocrites need Jesus, and they should be welcomed into any church hoping they find Jesus's transforming power. But to say the church being filled with hypocrites is a good thing, may be a bit of a stretch.

Imagine this: it is the time of ancient Greece when large groups of people would gather to watch the famous Greek plays. The actors would come out onto the stage and all the audience would cheer, "Here come the hypocrites!"

Yay! You bunch of sinners! No, they were not calling them sinners. They called the actors hypocrites because it meant 'someone who is pretending to be something they are not.' They were acting. The actors would wear masks and would even change their mask to play other parts or display a different emotion. They weren't actually angry, they just put on a mask to pretend to be angry for the part in the play.

So, it tracks that Jesus called the Pharisees hypocrites. He was saying they were pretending to follow God, but they were not actually following him. They acted like it, and from a distance it may be perceived that they were, but inside they were selfish, greedy, and filled with the bones of dead people.

I do not think it would be good for the church to be filled with people only pretending to follow Jesus. If it was, then everything would become superficial. People would feel obligated to keep up the charade and focus more on looking the part of 'Christian' than actually living like Christ. Acting like a Christian would be normalized and people wouldn't think twice about switching masks if needed for whatever situation they were in, so, from a distance, observers would think they were Christian.

If the church were full of hypocrites, you would see a shift in focus away from Christ. He would not need to be as important as tradition. The style of the worship service would become the prominent centerpiece. Oh, Christ would still be there, but he would be moved to the side. Groups would become more focused on how to worship properly rather than who they are worshiping. This focus would lead to arguments about whose tradition is better. Those arguments would lead to division. Those divisions would lead to more traditions. This cycle would repeat itself until there were 40,000 or more separate groups all calling themselves Christian.

I want to clarify here, I have often observed people confusing hypocrisy with falling short of Jesus's expectations. That results in thinking, "If a Christian sins, they are a hypocrite." But we all know Romans 3:23 (NASB), "All have sinned and fall short of the glory of God." So that cannot be right. A hypocrite is not someone who tries and fails. A hypocrite is someone who tries, fails, but pretends they succeeded. They wear a mask. They act.

I know I have failed many times over. I cannot pretend I haven't because so many people know about my failure. That is the difference. When we know we have sinned and fallen short of God's expectations, then we no longer have to pretend we are perfect and we can stop holding others to such high standards. Jesus called the Pharisees out on that too, "They tie up heavy, cumbersome loads and put them on other people's shoulders but they themselves are not willing to lift a finger to move them." —Matthew 23:4 (NIV).

There is a vast difference between someone doing their best to follow Jesus but falling short, and someone pretending to follow Jesus and pretending they do not fall short. The latter is a hypocrite. The former is human.

I can now stand and walk. I can even run—at least a little. A few weeks ago, I even went to a rock-climbing gym with my son and climbed to the top! By all outward appearances, I am fine. However, I still have massive amounts of internal damage that will take a long time to heal. One doctor told me the amount of soft tissue damage could take years to get back to normal.

Another doctor said I may never fully recover from all the internal injuries. There was nerve damage, ligament damage, and, of course, scarring. Scars tend to stick around for a long time.

This is not a negative projection. It is not a cry of "woe is me!" It is reality. It is true. I could try to pretend I am 100% healed and I could probably pull it off for a while. But if I stand or walk for too long, even sitting too long, it will take its toll on my body. I get very uncomfortable and eventually that will show through.

Interestingly, when we pretend we are perfectly following God, all the stuff we are hiding will eventually show through. When we hide the uncleanliness and decay that is lying just below the perfect white-washed exterior, someone will eventually notice it.

What is so difficult for many of us living this way is that we don't realize we don't have to live this way. We have an amazing God who loved us so much, even while we were standing opposed to him in our sinfulness, he sent his Son to save us from these sins. There is no need to hide them. We don't have to try to save face. We don't have to pretend we are perfect. That gets exhausting! It will drain the life out of you. Believe me, I have tried it!

In his book The Ragamuffin Gospel, Brennan Manning said, "The temptation of the age is to look good without being good." I want people to think I am doing fine, so I clean the outside of my cup and whitewash my tomb so I can present myself as whole, clean, and perfect while inside I am bitter, selfish, and angry.

The ancient proverb, "Medice, cura te ipsum—Physician, heal thyself" is such a tempting offer. If only I could show people I can be healed, then they will believe what I am saying. We think it will give credence to our message. And so, we fall prey to the temptation and act like we are healed. Then, when people respond to our message, it bolsters our hypocrisy and encourages us to continue the charade. But eventually, our mask falls, the whitewash fades, and the smell of rot and decay emanates from our insides. That is when we hear the accusations, "Hypocrite!"

The gospel I read in the Bible is a gospel of healing and restoration. It is not my responsibility to accomplish these things. I cannot heal myself! I am not my savior, nor am I yours. All I can do is be honest about my position in this life, whatever it may be, and give credit where credit is due. Jesus is my healer and savior!

One night at a youth camp, I saw one of my students slip out the back door of the chapel during an evening meeting. Concerned, I followed him. I found him weeping bitterly in the darkness. I comforted him and asked what was wrong. He told me he felt a strong burden for his friends at school but he was feeling the pressure of having to act like he was perfect around them because they knew he was a Christian. I said, "No! You don't have to do that. What you need to do is be honest with them. When you mess up, admit it! You will have more credibility by being honest than you will ever get by pretending to be perfect."

That is something we all need to hear! We do not have to pretend to be perfect! We are not perfect. In fact, 1 John 1:10 (NLT) says, "If we claim we have not sinned, we are calling God a liar and showing that his word has no place in our hearts." Pretending to be perfect will not help the gospel message. But honesty about our need for a savior will.

I appreciate how Rich Mullins addressed this during one of his concerts. He talked about how we don't sin by accident. We sin because we want to. We know what we are doing is wrong, but we choose to do it anyway. That is what makes it sinful. His take on this is applicable here, because even after we surrender our lives to him, we are still going to make terrible choices and sin. In these times, we need to be honest with people around us. More importantly, we need to be honest with ourselves. We need to be willing to admit what we did was wrong. We need to be humble enough to admit fault and apologize for our actions or words. We need to seek forgiveness and restoration with those we have offended.

If we put on airs and try to disguise or hide our sinfulness, we are adding another stroke of whitewash over our tomb. But we do not have to live this way. We can be free from our sinfulness by admitting it. People will try to hold things over our heads every time we fall short of God's glory. But guilt does not have to linger. Becoming a Christian does not remove our sinful deeds, but it does 'clean the inside of the cup.'

1 Peter 3:21 (ESV) says, "[Baptism is]...not as a removal of dirt from the body but as an appeal to God for a good conscience, through the resurrection of Jesus Christ." It is not just washing off the outside of the body! It is allowing God to clean our hearts as well. I have removed dirt from my body countless times so far. But, guess what, it just gets dirty again! But when God cleans me from the inside, he only has to do it once! Jesus died once for all sins. Any time I sin from now until the time I die has been covered by the blood of Christ! His grace does not allow the filth of sin to contaminate me any longer. This does not mean I am free to live however I want knowing Jesus has already covered my sins. But it does mean I do not have to try to cover my sins with whitewash!

We do not have to pretend to be perfect. We do not have righteousness of our own. It only comes from Christ. He is the one who washes us. We can only clean the outside of the cup, he can clean us inside and out!

The Hospital

*"A hospital bed is a parked taxi
with the meter running."*

—Groucho Marx

My trip to the hospital involved copious amounts of drugs
to help with the pain, which I'm sure it did. But it also caused a
bit of forgetfulness regarding the details of what all happened.
Most of my recollections are of lots of fast talking in terms I did
not necessarily understand, and lots of poking and prodding.

I was taken to our local emergency room where they
started a blood transfusion. Again, I just remember commotion
and people all around. I have no concept of how long I was in
the ER, but the next thing I recall is being wheeled out to a
helicopter.

Now, I have always dreamed of riding in a helicopter. This
was one of those life-long dreams and now I am barely
conscious for my first ride. It was very close quarters with the
three-person crew, my amazing wife, and me still strapped to
my rolling bed. It was not particularly uncomfortable other
than the throbbing pain in my core. I'm sure my adrenaline was
wearing off and the reality of what was happening started to set
in.

I remember resolving in my mind at about this point that I
was not going to make it up to camp that weekend and I would
need to find someone else to cover for me. The medical team

was continuing to give me blood on the trip to the closest hospital with a Level 1 Trauma ward. We made the 139 mile trip in about thirty minutes; Jennifer took a few short video clips and some photos from the flight. You know how you can pull memories from the depths of your brain from photos? I can vaguely recall some events from the flight after looking at the pictures. Some day, it would be nice to override those memories with a helicopter ride I actually choose to take.

When we arrived at our destination, they rushed me to a CT machine to assess the extent of my internal injuries. There were a couple of issues I had with this, and it had nothing to do with the enclosed space of the CT machine. First of all, I still had extreme pressure on my bladder. This is uncomfortable under normal circumstances, but added to the pain I was experiencing, it was terrible. That was not the worst part of my CT experience though. The biggest problem was that they had to remove the brace from my waist to put me into the machine. They used a cotton sheet as a binder tied tightly around my midsection, which I would stay in over the course of the next several days. This was the first time I remember having to be rolled over multiple times to get out of the brace and into the sheet.

It is very difficult to explain pain but I will do my best. I felt a combination of burning, stabbing, sharp, and throbbing pain all focused on the center of my body and radiating to the full extent of my extremities every time I was moved the tiniest amount. So when they rolled me over onto my side putting most of my weight on my hip, which, at the time, was not giving the support it is supposed to give, I howled in pain.

The CT scan was completed, and they sent me back to my room. They gave me a little remote control with one button on it that, supposedly, would administer pain-killing drugs when I pushed it. The button would light up green every ten minutes letting me know I could take another dose. I remember hitting the button as often as I could, but the pain was ever-present.

Now, keep in mind my accident happened on the Friday before July 4th. Also, keep in mind there are precious few orthopedic surgeons who are trained to repair open-book pelvic fractures, which is a very rare fracture (more on this later). So, I had to lie there four days waiting for the surgeon to return from vacation. There was a lot of button-pushing over those four days and not much else.

During this time of waiting, the only other activity I got to participate in was when the medical team had to come in and roll me on my side to tap on my spine and make sure I had not suffered a spinal injury. Let me set the scene. Several people would surround my bed, which had a mattress they could inflate with air. They would position themselves at strategic points on my framework to roll me to one side while another person would tap me from the top of my spine to the bottom the whole time asking me if I felt any pain where they were tapping.

Jennifer was able to catch one of these instances on video and showed it to me later. I was literally screaming with a completely contorted face, crying out in pain until I got onto my side, then my face would relax, and my brow unfurrowed and I said, almost calmly, "No pain. No pain. No pain..." until the doctor stopped poking me. I then resumed screaming, contorting my face as I was rolled back. This happened several times over the first twenty four-hours and was a wonderful addition to my memory bank.

Other than the rolling over and excruciating pain radiating through my body, the hospital stay was relatively comfortable. The food was not too bad, and the company was wonderful. I had several visitors who came in to see me, both family and friends. I even had a pastor come and pray with me. Well, just about everyone who visited prayed with me. In fact, my wife was getting texts from people half-way across the country who were praying for me on the first night we stayed in the hospital.

My wonderful wife, Jennifer, was with me the whole time. She slept on a tiny little couch, which I am sure was not very comfortable. I have no idea how much sleep she actually got. Between the hourly nurse visit, my moaning and groaning, and the ever-present beeping, it is amazing that she got any sleep at all.

Surgery came and went, and my condition stabilized. I still pushed the little green button as often as I noticed it light up. I will spare you details of my bodily functions. I will only mention they were not all functioning the way they ought. But, it was to be expected. After all, that part of my body absorbed most of the impact.

Lesson Learned

"They dress the wounds of my people
as though it were not serious.
'Peace, peace,' they say,
when there is no peace."
—Jeremiah 8:11 (NIV)

How often do we admit our struggles? How often do we fully rely on God and those around us for help through trouble, suffering, pain, grief, terrible choices, or any other struggle we might find ourselves in? On the other hand, how often do we convince ourselves that we are fine when we are not actually fine?

As I watched the video of me getting rolled over, it was obvious that I was in a lot of pain. Then something completely changed in my face, and even in my voice, "No pain. No pain. No pain!" The first time I watched the video I thought I was trying to convince myself I was not in pain. It took a while for me to realize I was actually telling the doctor I did not feel pain where he was poking me. But the entire scene was something I have not only witnessed, but often participated in week after week on Sunday mornings.

I would be grumpy, irritated, angry, or even in mental or physical anguish; but as soon as I step through the doors of the church, everything changes. My smile gets big enough for my teeth to show and I start lying through them! "I'm fine. I'm doing great! Happy to be here!" When, it may even be obvious that I am in anguish, hurting, or even angry. But I shake hands, smile, and act like nothing is wrong. Peace, peace, when there is no peace.

Now, medically speaking, I was telling the doctor the truth. I was not feeling pain where he was poking my spine. And this was a good thing. It indicated I was not actually suffering from a spinal injury. But watching it play out on the video Jennifer took showed me how ridiculous it looked to see the obvious pain and then the transition to "No pain."

James, the brother of Jesus, wrote a small book filled with awesome encouragement and challenges. One of them was that we ought to confess our sins to each other and pray for each other. This challenge goes beyond airing out our dirty laundry, or turning our sins into a brag session. But James goes on to say, "...so that you may be healed."

When we admit our struggles, we can then rely on the support of our Christian family to encourage us and lift us up in prayer. This allows us to bandage up the wounds rather than ignoring them and pretending that they are not serious.

"Bear one another's burdens, and so fulfill the law of Christ."—Galatians 6:2 (ESV). How can we do this if we do not know what each other's burdens are? When I just bottle up all my troubles, paste on a smile, and just pretend everything is fine, no one else will know I need help. It is normal to shy away from vulnerable situations, of course, but carrying my own burdens is not part of the gospel message.

The main problem with this type of behavior is that it is expected, and often promoted within "church culture." I don't want you to tell me what you are struggling with because then I would feel obligated to do something about it. Since I don't really want to actually have to help you, I encourage you to keep your troubles to yourself. I certainly am not going to bother you with my problems, so why would I want you to bother me with yours?

Then our wounds fester, get infected, and eventually cause problems. This can result in sudden outbursts, angry interactions, jealousy within the church body, partiality, slander, gossip, withholding grace and mercy, unforgiveness, division, and disunity! I only know this because I have experienced it, ashamedly, from both sides. I was the one who let unhealed pains lead me to treat others, whom I called my family in Christ, like the scum of the earth. And I have been on the receiving end of this type of treatment as well. Neither side is a pleasant experience.

Holding on to grudges is not protecting yourself. It is actually a form of self-harm. Allowing others to help us with our burdens brings healing. We no longer expend all our energy trying to protect ourselves. It is exhausting putting up a facade. Our hurts and pains, constantly weighing on us, leave us physically and mentally depleted.

Now, if you are holding things over other people's heads, you need to repent, apologize, and release that person from the trap you created around them. It is not your responsibility to make sure others pay for their sins. Remember, Jesus already paid for them. Though you may have a desire—and even a need—to see someone pay for what they put you through, that is not our position, nor our right.

This does not mean we can just allow anyone to treat us anyway they want and roll over and take it. While we are not allowed to hold a grudge, you need to have boundaries. Boundaries are healthy and good, not just for the offended, but for the offenders as well. These boundaries are often just what is needed for healing to take place for both individuals. For example, picture an open wound. Now picture it bandaged up. We put a boundary around it to allow it to heal.

There has to be a balance between blurting out every terrible experience or sin and hiding everything deep inside, hoping no one will ever notice. Understanding this balance is difficult, especially within the open setting of a public worship service. We can smile and shake people's hands. We can even tell people we are doing ok, even if there are underlying struggles we are dealing with. The only stipulation I would add to that would be telling people we are ok—even if we are struggling—is fine as long as we have a healthy outlet for those underlying struggles. Find a trusted friend, someone you look up to for their character and honesty and be honest with them.

Here's the thing: we all know that no one is perfect. We can stop pretending we are perfect and that we expect the same from everyone else. Imagine the relief of not having to hold up that pretense. We are all human and we all make poor choices. What differentiates a Christian trying their best to follow Christ from a hypocrite is honesty. Honesty with themselves and with those around them. A hypocrite will deny, deflect, accuse, and attempt to turn everything around on others. A Christian will admit when they were wrong. They will apologize and seek forgiveness and restoration. That is the difference between someone with a hardened heart and someone after God's own heart.

Find someone to open up to. Allow others a safe place for them to open up to you. Find peace. Find healing.

My Darkest Night

"You lock the door
And throw away the key
There's someone in my head
but it's not me"

—Pink Floyd, George Roger Waters
Dark Side of the Moon, Brain Damage (1973)

Overall, my stay at the hospital was pretty good, despite all the pain and screaming. The staff was great and kept me on the mend...well, all except for one. This particular night was definitely the worst experience I have ever had in a hospital—or anywhere, really. The nurse who came in to take care of my evening routine that night must have been trained at a torture chamber. She was extremely rough with my cleaning, rolling me around like a rag doll, and she literally ripped one of my IVs out. This was such a traumatic experience that my wife called in the charge nurse and requested another nurse take over.

That was not the worst part of the night. It was probably a combination of the disquieting events and the drugs, but whatever caused it, I hope to experience nothing like it ever again. On this side of it, it almost seems humorous. And I have laughed about it, but only to the extent of recalling just how chilling it was.

I woke up with a start and it was pitch black. I realized someone had moved me into a new room. Everything was deathly silent. My breathing quickened immediately. I must have cried out because Jennifer was almost instantly by my side and had the lights turned on quickly. Now, with the lights on, I was sure someone had moved to a new location. The nurse came in and I didn't recognize her. I began to feel anxious.

I looked over at the window, and it had been blacked out! There was, literally, nothing out the window, just blackness. I tried to turn from side to side, but felt like I was tied to the bed. And then panic set in. I was sure "they" had switched my nurse with someone, but who, and why??

I asked where I was. The "nurse" told me I was in the same room I had always been in—of course she would say that, she was one of "them!" But then Jennifer assured me it was true.

The voice in my head was almost a scream, "Oh, no! They had altered her too!" Now sheer terror had overwhelmed my feeble mind and I was gasping for breath.

Somehow, a construct had developed in my mind overpowering reality. Some government agency had drugged and transported me to an underground facility where they were, obviously, running medical tests on me. This was so real it took my wife quite a while to put me at ease. Thinking back now, I am amazed at how real it felt. I was not just suspicious that this had happened to me; I knew it!

After I had calmed down, I asked for confirmation. I went so far as to request they run some tests to see what drug was given to me. I had Jennifer take pictures of the parts of the room I couldn't see in an attempt to verify it was the same room. Needless to say, they had not drugged me (other than the pain medication I was on) and I was, indeed, still in the same room I was in the night before...or so 'they' say!

Lesson Learned

*"The realm of fairy-story is wide and deep
and high and filled with many things:
all manner of beasts and birds are found there;
shoreless seas and stars uncounted;
beauty that is an enchantment,
and an ever-present peril;
both joy and sorrow as sharp as swords."
—J. R. R. Tolkien, Tolkien On Fairy-stories*

It is truly amazing what our minds can imagine. Our brains are created in the image of a creator, so it goes without saying there is creativity inside every one of us—latent as it may be. God designed us to have imaginations and gave us the ability to dream. Sometimes, though, our imagination leads us astray, and we convince ourselves that something is true, even when it isn't.

2 Timothy 4:3-4 (NIV) says this:

> *For the time will come when people*
> *will not put up with sound doctrine.*
> *Instead, to suit their own desires,*
> *they will gather around them a great*
> *number of teachers to say what their*
> *itching ears want to hear. They will*
> *reject the truth and chase after*
> *myths.*

This verse is often used to try to get 'you' (the one who evidently rejected the truth) to think like 'me' (the one who obviously has the truth). But the author, Paul, was even willing to admit when he was wrong. Our mind can deceive us and convince us we are right about one thing or another, even if it is the furthest thing from the truth. More often, though, we are just a tiny bit to one side or another from the truth. That way, there is enough truth in our stance that the tiny amount we are off doesn't seem to be too far off.

Now, this chapter is not about establishing which doctrine is true and which is not. However, as I reflected on this darkest night in the hospital, I couldn't help but think about times I had argued tooth-and-nail for or against a certain doctrine only to eventually change my mind later. Some would call this waffling and accuse me of capitulation; but I am certain we all have changed our mind on what we believe about God or his Word at least once in our faith journey.

The "seat of emotion" is a term that refers to where our decisions and emotions originate within our body. Is it our heart or mind? Over the years there have been many differing ideas as to where these decisions and emotions come from. Think of common phrases we know.

"I love you with all my heart."
"I have a gut feeling."
"I feel it in my bones."

The Bible even refers to the bowels as the seat of emotion. Of course, as we now know, the amygdala—part of our limbic system—is where we process environmental input and produce responses, or emotions. This is a microcosm of what happens in our spiritual life. We think the heart holds our emotion because we can feel physical stimuli in our chest during emotional times. Then we started connecting our gastrointestinal activity with excitement or depression. But then, as science progressed and brain scans became ubiquitous, we came to understand more about where these emotions seem to originate.

Who knows, a thousand years from now, some scientist might discover a nerve connected to the amygdala that goes all the way down to the big toe, and there will be another shift in understanding. People will express love with toe-shaped chocolates!

So, did the truth change? Did the seat of emotion actually move around in some evolutionary migration of the soul? Not at all. Our understanding changed.

The problem most of us face during these drastic changes is that wherever we are in our level of understanding God and his scripture, we believe it to be the truth. Therefore, if we believe it, that makes it 'truth'! Circular logic? Why—Yes, and our brain tells us it is true even if it is not. We all have experienced this on some level. We may have been deceived by someone we trusted or unintentionally received misinformation that made us believe a lie. And we all know the feeling when we realize what we thought was 'truth' is not actually 'truth.'

There has been a trend lately where people who have been Christians all their lives give up on their faith. They call it deconstruction, where they break down the fundamental building blocks of their faith and determine it was all wrong.

The only thing I can tell you about these situations is that their faith was built on something other than Jesus Christ. Their loyalties were with something other than God's kingdom.

I was a youth pastor for several years. I noticed over the years kids raised in the church were leaving the church at increasing rates. This alarmed me so much that I started researching the statistics. I saw year-over-year as kids "aged out" of the youth group they were leaving the church. I found this fascinating and tried to figure out how we could get these kids plugged in to another program or other group to keep them in church.

That's when it hit me. They didn't need another program. They didn't need "young adult" activity groups. They didn't need "connect" groups. They didn't need volunteer opportunities. I realized we were spending so much time and effort connecting them to "church" and so little energy connecting them to Jesus. Now, don't get me wrong, I am not saying we need to abandon all programs and activities. That is not my point.

My point is, it would be a mistake to think that in connecting folks to the church we are inherently connecting them to Jesus. We often think getting people into a church building will connect people to Jesus, and sometimes it does work that way. But one of my favorite Bible verses tells me a different story. "Follow my example, as I follow the example of Christ." —1 Corinthians. 11:1 (NIV).

We can *tell* people about Jesus until we are blue in the face. What they need is for us to *show* them Jesus. When people ask us what it means to follow Jesus, we should be able to say, "come spend the day with me and I will show you." Our *daily walk* is where the proverbial rubber hits the road. That is where what we really believe to be true is played out.

I have often thought, and shared from many pulpits, the biggest problem the North American church faces is that we do not believe what we say we believe. That is why deconstruction works. That is why people are leaving their faith. That is why church attendance in America is on a seventy-year decline. That is why far fewer Americans are self-proclaimed Christians today compared to five years ago. Many of us have established a social religion based on several moral standards and platitudes instead of the life-giving, life-changing, and freeing gospel of Jesus Christ.

We place our faith in organizations rather than God. We follow popular Christian influencers instead of the Holy Spirit. We honor a moral code instead of honoring our Lord and Savior. We do not take the time to get connected to Jesus. I know this to be true, because if we were really connected to him, we wouldn't leave. The fact that people are walking away is a good indication that they were connected to the wrong thing.

The critical reader might be thinking, "You can't say that because you don't know people's hearts." However, Jesus told us we can know people by the fruit they are producing. (Matthew 7:20)

What about the years of studying scripture these people have and they still walk away? Knowing 'about' Jesus and knowing Jesus are two very different things. I can know 'about' something just by reading books or listening to a teacher. But I won't truly know it until I experience it. I have read a lot about the Grand Canyon and I am fascinated by it. However, I have never been there so I have not experienced the Grand Canyon; I just attained information about it. Experience—or maturity— comes when we combine the information with action. Information leads to mental ascent, but not necessarily to experience.

We have lived in this culture for so long that Christianity has all-but dwindled to an exchange of information; head-knowledge moving from one brain to another. Matthew 7:22-23 tells us that many people think they are following Jesus. They think they are on the right path. But when it comes down to it, Jesus tells them, "I never knew you." This possibility scares me worse than my waking nightmare in the hospital did.

I was absolutely sure of every detail of my situation. I knew what had happened. I knew I had been drugged and hauled to an underground bunker. There was no question in my mind...until there was. I had created a reality. I had turned a few little morsels of truth into a horror story. But it was all an illusion created inside my brain.

Our brains are powerful things. They can complete innumerable calculations in an instant, create amazing art, design beautiful landscapes, develop practical ideas, and establish timeless constructs. All this within a mass of grey matter we refer to as our mind, and our minds can change. As I said earlier, I have changed my mind on all kinds of things I once held as solid truth. I am sure we have all done this.

Many times these changes come from maturity or a better understanding of a particular verse. Whether we contribute this to strong argumentation or our keen intellect, I can assure you it is not by your own power you are enlightened to the things of God. 1 Corinthians 2:10b-12 (NLT) tells us that God reveals his mysteries to us through the power of his Spirit. It says:

> For his Spirit searches out everything and shows us God's deep secrets. No one can know a person's thoughts except that person's own spirit, and no one can know God's thoughts except God's own Spirit. And we have received God's Spirit (not the world's spirit), so we can know the wonderful things God has freely given us.

I do not have a corner on the truth. The pastor of my church does not have a corner on the truth. The denomination I belong to does not have a corner on the truth. God is the only one who knows all truth. The rest of us just make stuff up as we go along and convince ourselves it is true. That is, until, little by little, God's Spirit reveals to us where we are wrong. And, little by little, we conform to the truth of God's word until one day when we will eventually be glorified into new beings through the power of the Holy Spirit, who is chipping away at our carnal minds. At that point we are no longer "seeing in a mirror, dimly, but...face to face..." and we will know as we are known (1 Corinthians 13:12). Then—and only then—can we say we have all the truth. We will stand before God and all the lies of our life will melt away revealing the only thing left—truth!

Paul, who wrote the verse above, goes on to explain in 1 Corinthians chapter 3 that after the foundation of truth is laid in our lives, we build on it. Some of us use cheap material, and others use expensive stuff, but eventually everything we use to build on that foundation will be put to the test of fire. Once everything burns away through this refining process, only truth will remain.

Don't fake your way through this Christian life. Don't give in to the pop-culture of Christian Moralism, or grab the low-hanging fruit of easy-believism. This life is too short to wait to make your faith real! This doesn't mean we just need to redouble our efforts in studying scripture, re-read our favorite devotionals, listen to more sermons, or attend a seminary. All those are good, but, by themselves, will only increase our knowledge. We also must humble ourselves before God and submit to his Spirit's guidance. That path leads to understanding and maturity. Then we are able to follow Paul's instructions to Timothy, "Do your best to present yourself to God as one approved, a worker who has no need to be ashamed, rightly handling the word of truth."

Rehab

I tried to find out who actually said this first, but it has been accredited to so many different people that it is really hard to tell. I first saw the phrase on a tee shirt in the "late nineteen-hundreds" (I'm glad this phrase exists now!). But, I am here to tell you—rehab is definitely not for quitters.

After my surgery, the surgeon told me I would be 100% non-weight-bearing for a minimum of three months. They told me I had to give my bones time to heal before putting any pressure on my hips and tailbone. I was warned to follow these instructions specifically if I expected to walk again. Of course, they assured me a full recovery was expected, but the surgeon's warning stuck with me. I did not want to be in a wheelchair for the rest of my life, so I was determined to follow all the doctor's orders. So, for the next three months, I was either lying down or sitting.

Here is the down-side, the human body cannot be in any position where it does not put pressure on its hips or tailbone. Not sitting, lying down, standing on your head, or any other position! I was in constant pain and I could not get comfortable.

The hospital sent me to an inpatient rehabilitation center. It was exactly the same as being in the hospital except for the care team. I simply traded nurses for therapists. They came in twice a day to teach me how to move myself from a lying down position into a wheelchair. Because I was not allowed to put any weight on my feet, I used a slide board—it was about two-and-a-half feet long and eight inches wide. I placed one end of the board on the edge of the bed and the other on the edge of my wheelchair and then shifted my weight, using only my arms, across the board and into the chair.

The therapists also taught me how to dress, bathe, and complete other necessary procedures. They equipped me with all kinds of tools, utensils, and adaptable furniture. I had to use a shower chair and a commode stool. These were a challenge to navigate at first, but I got used to it quickly.

I had another set of therapists who focused solely on getting my strength and range of motion back. You would be surprised at how painful it can be to stretch ligaments that have been dormant for two weeks. But, I remembered my orders to listen to the doctors so I wouldn't have to stay in the wheelchair any longer than necessary.

The wheelchair was a totally different story. Once I got into the chair, which was an incredibly exhausting feat at first, the world was my oyster. The staff was very surprised at how quickly I adapted to navigating with my new-found transportation. So I had to share my secret. I have always been fascinated by wheelchairs. From when I was very young, I always wondered what it would be like to be confined to one, so I practiced. Whenever I had the opportunity, I would sit in one and wheel myself around. I got quite good at riding wheelies and doing spins. The therapists, however, negated my exuberance and told me not to attempt either of the latter two. At least not in the halls.

So, over the next several days, I learned to live with new accoutrements; grabbers, hooks, scrubbers on a stick, slide boards, commode stools, shower chairs, and the whole bit. It was like being a child again. Starting over. Learning to use muscles that had been forgotten—stretching, rolling, and shuffling my body around with unnatural methods. And all of this was just to use the bathroom.

My mornings quickly developed a routine. I would shower (or sponge bathe), complete bathroom needs, change clothes, and have breakfast. At first, these activities included a therapist who coached me every step of the way. I'll have to admit, it is very humbling re-learning basic functions as an adult.

I would often get a break between breakfast and my first therapy session. So I would either get back into bed for a rest—morning routines were often exhausting—or I would sit in my chair and read or watch some TV. But other days I would go straight from breakfast to the physical therapy room. The room was filled with all-kinds of equipment and contraptions used to treat various types of injuries. I found out later most physical therapy results from surgery.

The therapist would wheel me in and I would 'slide' onto a huge padded table. I would then work on my exercises. What I could do was pretty limited because of the doctor's restrictions, however, the sets were extremely challenging the first time I did them. I had ankle flexes, leg lifts (but with a bolster under the back of my knee so I was only lifting from the knee down), glute flexes, heel slides (sliding my heel up toward my butt), and the most painful of them all was abduction and adduction (legs fully extended and sliding them out as far as I could and then back in like the bottom half of a snow angel). Of course all of these exercises were completed while lying flat on my back.

I did not know it at the time, but my leg muscles would lose over seventy-five percent of their strength over the next three months. My therapists constantly stressed the importance of keeping it up. They told stories of people who were perfectly capable of walking again, but didn't keep up with their assigned regiment, which prolonged the recovery and made walking extremely painful. Looking back now, it was well worth the effort.

Lesson Learned

"When Christ calls a man,
He bids him come and die."
—Dietrich Bonhoeffer

This quote has become a large part of my understanding of what it means to follow Christ. It is taken from Bonhoeffer's book, "The Cost of Discipleship." Here I was, lying on my back, working through my therapy session because I had counted the cost of what would happen if I didn't do them. Straining through yet another set of abductions, my thick skull made the connection to counting the cost of following Christ.

I was raised in the church. My father was a preacher. I rarely missed a church service. I was taught how to read by using Bible verses. So how did I miss the fact that Jesus was calling me to give up everything about myself to be his follower? To me, counting the cost meant realizing if I didn't follow Jesus, I would burn in hell, and I really didn't want that. So, I followed Jesus—or so I thought.

Sure, I went through all the proper motions of what everyone else did. I listened to Christian music, read Christian fiction books, I even wore Christian clothes! You know, the shirts that ripped off popular logos and added a Christian catch-phrase? Like the Mountain Dew logo that said "Meant to Die" or the orange shirt with "Jesus" scrawled in Reese's font? Even though I talked, walked, and dressed like a Christian, my loyalties were still with myself. I still lived my life the way I wanted to. I made my own choices. I was the ruler of my own domain.

I should start a little further back, just to give you an idea of how I came to know Jesus and turn my life over to him. It started at a very young age. As I already stated, my education included Bible teaching and Christian traditions. I attended a private school in the basement of the church my family attended. To top it off, my dad was the principal, my teacher, and my preacher! Bible memorization was a central part of the curriculum across all subjects. Even outside of church, the Christian culture of the 1980s and 1990s surrounded me.

In our traditions, the church services included serving communion every week at every service. But you had to be a "Christian" in order to take communion. Also, if you were a Christian, they would let you volunteer to serve communion! I was nine years old when I told my dad I wanted to become a Christian. My dad wanted to make sure I knew what I was deciding to do, so he asked me several questions about my decision. That is when my Christian education kicked in. I knew all the right answers—or at least the answers I knew my dad was looking for—because that is what I was taught. For example, "Why do you want to commit your life to Christ?" My automatic response was, "Because He is my Lord and Savior." Which is the right answer; I just had no idea what it meant.

Since I got all the questions 'right,' my dad decided I understood. Another part of our traditions included baptism as a part of committing one's life to Christ. After talking with my dad for a while I asked if I could get baptized. The baptism took place in a horse tank filled just for that purpose, and there were several families from the church there to celebrate the event.

Now for a little behind-the-scenes look into my brain when all this went down. As I mentioned before, you had to be a 'Christian' to serve communion. One of my friends, a classmate at our Christian school, had made the decision to be baptized earlier that week and told me about it. I realized he would be able to serve communion to the whole church and I wasn't! I also wanted to serve communion, so I asked to be baptized too.

Having everyone around and confessing my desire to follow Jesus was an incredible experience, and I believe I meant it. Again, I just did not know what I was getting into. I had a head full of information, but no experience to back it up—I had no maturity. But how much maturity can you really expect from a nine-year-old boy?

Back to the story. The very next Sunday, my friend and I were serving communion. I got what I wanted and everyone seemed happy about it. I cruised through the next several years without much of a hitch. Other than the occasional unruliness, oh, and the fact that now I had to hide all my sinfulness from everyone so that I continued to look like a Christian. Because, we all know, you can't sin and call yourself a Christian...right?

Needless to say, I had developed some very unhealthy ideas around what it meant to be a Christian. As I got into my teen years, I started acting out, probably for attention, and was quickly pegged as a rebellious Preacher's Kid, aka a PK. From that point forward, I resolved to live up to my reputation. I acted how I wanted when no one was around, but then pasted on my Christian face while I was around Christians. One night the police came knocking at our door and this balancing act became very difficult. I had made some terrible choices and got caught.

One of the men of the church came to our house and sat with my dad and I. This man scolded me, and told me I would have to get up in front of the whole church and confess my sins. He said I wouldn't be allowed to serve communion anymore. He convinced me I wasn't truly a Christian at that point. I certainly had not been acting like one. I couldn't figure out why. What went wrong? I did everything I was taught to do. The only thing my teen-aged brain could come up with was that I must have messed up the formula for being saved—I had done part of it wrong. But which part? It must have been the baptism! So I figured I might as well try it again. Maybe this time it would take!

It didn't.

I was, however, a lot more careful about getting caught. Because, WOW! That was embarrassing. I never wanted to have to get up in front of a church again just to 'confess my sins.' I do not think that was what James had in mind when he encouraged us to confess our sins to each other. Besides, what I went through did not lead to healing, just bitterness and self-loathing.

I was attending a youth camp not long after this whole thing went down and the theme was "Passing the Torch." A few older preachers were asking teens to come forward and commit to being a preacher. Now, I have never heard God speak to me in an audible voice, but he has made things very clear to me over the years. At this point, I knew God was calling me to go up on stage and make the commitment. Instead I, literally grabbed hold of the bench in front of me and refused to move. I could recall the things I saw my father go through as a preacher, and I wanted nothing to do with that.

Now, fast forward about a decade. I am married with a daughter and a son on the way. The pastor of the church we were attending had recognized some qualities in me and encouraged me to develop my preaching abilities. I took his advice and began doing some fill-in preaching at various churches who did not have their own pastor. After preaching at one of those churches, they asked me to come and be their pastor. I was gobsmacked—or should I say, God-smacked. I had been running from this idea for ten plus years and this job offer fell into my lap.

If you will recall, I am not a huge proponent of the idea that God has a specific calling for each individual's life, but I could not argue with him on this anymore. I accepted the position and entered vocational ministry.

I do not intend to brag here, but I was good at preaching. Seeking out tough issues, I challenged the status quo. I enjoyed bringing up controversial doctrines and debating difficult theologies. I read and studied, studied and read, and listened to sermons every day to brush up on topics. But, unfortunately, I turned preaching into *my* platform rather than God's. I was angry with 'church' and fed up with hypocrisy. After dealing with inconsistencies in church teaching all my life, *I* was going to put a stop to it!

I was preaching for two years at this church when one of the elders pulled me aside and challenged me with something I will never forget. He said, "It seems like the church you grew up in hurt you, and now you are taking it out on us." That hit me squarely between the eyes. He was exactly right. This elder lovingly pointed out my error, and I thank God for prompting this man to bring it to my attention.

Until then, I thought I was doing the work of God. I felt justified in my self-righteousness. From that point forward, I started looking more closely at scripture. I started focusing on the heart of my preaching. I realized I was asking people to do something I have never done. I was challenging them to leave off their devotion to self and turn their allegiance over to Christ. I went through the actions of "becoming a Christian" but I never gave my life to him!

The whole reason I shared this story of my struggle through my relationship with God is so your struggle does not need to be as hard! Learn from my poor choices rather than your own. I also want to encourage you, especially if you have had similar experiences.

I did not sit down and calculate the cost of following Christ. Instead, I relied on my own understanding of what it meant to follow Jesus. In doing so, I injured my relationship with God almost to the point of ruining it. Not on His part! No, every time I felt distant from God it was because I had moved further away from Him! The damage I did to that relationship required mending. It required painful stretching of my understanding and exercising of my faith. It took a lot of hard work to rebuild what was broken!

Now my relationship with Jesus is stronger than ever. Sure, I still battle with self-loyalty and egotism, but I know my place before my God. I know I am going to mess things up again, but I also know we serve a God of restoration! I know I will still make poor choices, but I know God is bigger than my choices. I know my performance is not going to be good enough, but I know my standing before God is not based on my performance. "My dear children, I am writing these things to you so that you will not sin. But if anyone does sin, we have an advocate before the Father—Jesus Christ, the Righteous One." —1 John 2:1 (BSB).

Please, count the cost of following Jesus. Know what you are getting into. Don't rely on your own understanding, but become broken before God. Humble yourself. Seek him. Know him. Allow him to know you —he already knows you better than you know yourself! It is worth it to know where you stand in comparison to an almighty and sovereign God!

The Realization

*"We are not as strong
as we think we are."*

*—Rich Mullins, David Strasser
Songs (1996)*

I was glad to be discharged from rehab. Some amazing friends had taken a Saturday to come to our house and build a ramp so I could get inside with my wheelchair. My father-in-law even widened one of our doorways to accommodate me and my new wheels. I had a hospital bed set up in our living room with a trapeze over it to assist with scooting around in bed.

I have heard the phrase "adaptable" when referring to modification to assist individuals with disabilities. Now I understood what that meant. I certainly had to adapt, and my family had to adapt. Even my environment had to adapt. This was a tough situation. I could not do all the things I had once done for myself. I had become very dependent on my family, especially my wife.

The hospital had assigned an occupational therapist to visit me and make sure our home was 'adaptable' enough for me with my newfound limitations. She talked through a lot of my exercises and routines and how they would need to be altered based on my environment. After all the formalities, she said candidly, "I have only seen one other case like yours and I have been doing this for over thirty years." She then told me about her father who was elderly and had fallen off a horse and suffered the same injuries I had suffered.

Now, during my hospital stay, and even in rehab, I heard similar comments. How I was the 'youngest patient they had with this injury,' or 'you don't see many bounce back from this like you did.' Even comments about being able to walk again. In my head, I was stuck on the age thing. I thought this injury must be unique only in the fact that I am in my mid-forties and broke my hip. I had no idea they were talking about the severity of my injuries.

But after the therapist left that day I started thinking about it more and decided to look up my injuries on the internet. I was shocked! I read: open-book pelvic fracture...blah, blah, (technical medical descriptions)...are "potentially lethal due to associated injuries and massive pelvic hemorrhaging."(nih. gov). What! Potentially lethal?

I continued searching. I found, "Open-book dislocation of the pubic symphysis are rare, representing 0.3-8.2% of all fractures, and can lead to fatal complications through vascular, abdominal, and nervous injuries." (jetem.org) I had no idea just how life threatening my situation had been! That was when I realized why so many of my caregivers were so surprised. It wasn't that I was young, it was that I actually survived my injuries!

My realizations did not end there. The officer who was first on the scene still had some of my personal belongings and had told my wife to call when he could stop by and drop them off. Once we were home again, we called to set up a time for him to drop by. We got to chatting a little and I asked him about the scene of the accident. He stated very clearly, "It did not make sense."

He described the physics of an automobile accident and where I should have ended up. He described his surprise that I was not bloodied at all. He had seen a lot of accidents over his career and this did not compare.

From the very moment of my accident, I knew God had protected me. In-fact, I was very vocal about it with everyone I talked to. "Wow! You were lucky!" they would say after hearing I was not wearing a helmet.

"Luck had nothing to do with it. It was all God," was my typical reply.

But now I realized God hadn't simply protected me. He had, actually, spared me! There were so many indications I never realized. I knew people were praying for me. I knew I lost a lot of blood and needed a transfusion. I heard the doctors and nurses talking about how rare it was. I never put it all together until this moment.

I should not have survived! Yet I did!

Lesson Learned

"Where, O death, is your victory?
Where, O death, is your sting?"
—1 Corinthians 15:55 (NIV)

Death is such an interesting thing. Most of us have at least given it some thought, and many are afraid of it. One thing is for sure, it will continue to happen until God returns to redeem his creation. The mortality rate of humans, so far, is 100%. I do not state this to be macabre—it is just a fact—but macabre is a really fun word to say!

As a pastor, I saw a lot of death. I wept with those who wept and mourned with those who mourned. I performed funeral services for people I had never met in person. I also spent time with people who knew they were dying and prayed with them during their last days. I had no idea being around so much death was not normal.

Knowing death is one breath closer does not soften its blow when it happens. It is certainly devastating and can cause a person to deal with grief for the rest of their life. It is normal and healthy to grieve. Working through emotions is a necessary step to help you wrap your mind around a person who is no longer there, especially when they were a crucial part of your life.

I am sharing all this about death up front so you can understand my position. We can be sad when someone we love dies, and we cannot avoid grief. However, we do not need to let death have the victory. Death is not the final event. I absolutely believe in an afterlife. There are those reading this who may have already developed opinions on the afterlife—or lack thereof. I am not here to press my opinions on anyone, but I do want to acknowledge my ideas are only opinions. I have never visited the afterlife and have no firsthand knowledge of anyone who has and returned to tell the tale.

Of course, I have read the accounts and stories of people who spent how-ever-many minutes or days in heaven and were revived after being pronounced dead. I am not trying to dispute or argue with anyone, but I have never died and seen the other side. So I cannot tell you anything about it other than what I read in scripture. 1 Corinthians 2:9 (NLT) tells us, "...no eye has seen, no ear has heard, and no mind has imagined what God has prepared for those who love him."

Death does not have to have the final say in life. I fully believe when this life is over we will enter into another life—an eternal life! I believe this body of mine is now susceptible to pain, suffering, and, yes, even death! My Bible describes a new heaven and a new earth, restored, redeemed, and incorruptible. We will also be given new bodies. What will they look like? I have no idea, but it will be awesome!

Where am I going with all of this? I know it is easy to focus on this life. The day-to-day events tend to keep our attention. When they don't, we often think about the next day's activities, or the next. Sometimes, we even borrow worries from the future, just so we have something to occupy our minds today. This is normal. But Jesus calls us to be different.

Pastor Craig Groeschel goes so far as to say that Jesus' followers ought to be weird. In his book, Weird: Because Normal isn't Working, he says, "Don't settle for a normal life. Not when you can enjoy the wonderful weirdness of being who God created you to be." It would be weird if we didn't worry about stuff. It would be weird if we were not completely focused on this life. It would be weird if our finances, schedule, debt, or entertainment didn't fill every waking thought—and even the sleeping ones! It would be weird if we didn't fear death!

The Apostle Paul, in 1 Corinthians 15:54-56 (ESV), says:

> *When the perishable puts on the imperishable and the mortal puts on immortality, then shall come to pass the saying that was written: 'Death is swallowed up in victory. Where, O death, is your victory? Where, O death, is your sting?' The sting of death is sin, and the power of sin is the law. But thanks be to God who gives us the victory through Jesus Christ our Lord.*

Death is not the end!

Another point we need to remember is this life is not the only thing we were promised. Scripture has a little to say on this point as well. 1 Corinthians 15:19 (NLT) tells us, "...if our hope in Christ is only for this life, we are more to be pitied than anyone in the world."

Jesus even said in John 16:33 (NIV), "I told you these things so that in me you may have peace. In this world you will have trouble. But take heart! I have overcome the world." What was it he told them so they could have peace? Well, he just finished saying they will be scattered and run away leaving Jesus all alone. What?! How does that give them peace?

Sometimes, knowing what is going to happen allows us to handle things better. Or, at least, it allows us more opportunity to process the situation. I am a chicken when it comes to scary movies. I will readily admit it. Jump scares—well—they scare me! My wife quickly found this out on our honeymoon. We sat down to watch a psychological thriller. I like the genre, but I don't like the scary parts. I sat on the couch and grabbed a pillow, which I would methodically hold to my face during scary parts. My brand new wife sat there laughing at me as I peeked over the pillow during a particularly intense scene.

Here's the kicker. Once I have watched the scary movie (and survived) I would eagerly watch it a second or third time! It wasn't that I didn't get scared anymore, I just knew what to expect. Sometimes the pillow came out during second viewings, but often just a blanket worked. Then, during the third viewing, I was fine! Well, not really, but by then I could anticipate the scenes and time glances around the room or at my watch to keep safe from the jump scenes. I can freely confess this now, because I am sure no-one I know will ever read this, so I'm sure I am safe from any embarrassment.

Movies are not the only things that scare me. I was a pastor for over a decade. I preached hundreds of sermons in front of hundreds of people at a time. And I am afraid of public speaking! Ask my wife. It doesn't matter if it is the first time or the hundredth time I get up in front of a crowd; I get nervous. My palms sweat, my mouth gets dry, I fidget with stuff in my pocket, and an endless list of nervous ticks and quirks violently spring to the surface.

The American Psychological Association has published research that shows the number one fear in the US was the fear of public speaking, and the second most common fear was death (Dwyer & Davidson (2012) https://www.apa.org/pubs/

journals/releases/dev-dev0000548.pdf). This means there are people who would rather die than get up to speak in front of people. Granted, I am not that afraid of public speaking, but I do still get nervous. Also, I am not sure if these were accurate statistics or not, but they make a good point.

Another friend encouraged me in my fear of public speaking. It wasn't the typical "face your fears" type of speech (which ironically can often cause more harm than good). Instead, he told me it wasn't a matter of overcoming the fear, but rather managing the symptoms. He told me to watch a video of my sermons or speeches and take note of all the ticks and quirks. He had me listen intently to the audio as well. Once he made me count how many times I used filler words, like "uh" and "um." That was humbling! But it equipped me to deal with my actions and words that were direct results of my fear. I had no idea how distracting those types of idiosyncrasies were. They can take away so much from a message, no matter how poignant or compelling the points are. If the speaker is bumbling over his words it is hard to take them seriously.

After following my friend's advice, I had some idea of some things to work on. Two simple steps I took were: 1. I stopped keeping things in my pockets, and 2. I cut back on using filler words. I never fully overcame the fear of getting up in front of people, but I was able to make it look like I had. This is very different from hypocrisy (pretending to be something you aren't) because I will readily admit to being afraid, even while I am standing on stage. Sometimes it even helps me to relax a bit—just acknowledging my fear. Knowing what to expect equipped me to make changes so my sermons could be better. I never became a famous orator (not yet anyway) but I was, at least, more tolerable to listen to. I'd love to say I stopped sweating beforehand, but I still do.

So where does that leave us regarding death? Can I say we ought to know what to expect? Not exactly. But we know one thing. It is coming. In the words of The Flaming Lips, "Do you realize that everyone you know someday will die?" Death is something we can count on; however we don't have to face this alone.

The good new is: Jesus died for us. We all know those verses in Romans that tell us "all have sinned" and "the wages of sin is death." Hebrews says, Jesus died once for all. We do not have to fear death. We can have confidence that death will be destroyed (1 Corinthians 15:26). Death will not have the final say.

I like the way C. S. Lewis put it. In his book 'Till We Have Faces' he wrote, "Death opens a door out of a little, dark room (that's all the life we have known before it) into a great, real place where the true sun shines and we shall meet." Not only will we be in the presence of our maker, we will be surrounded by a great cloud of others who got there before we did. My Bible describes an amazing reunion with a banquet! This is not some far-off intangible enigma. No! It will be real food we can taste! Friends and loved ones we can embrace!

I have not become some enlightened guru who has no fear, but when it became apparent to me I was going to hit the other vehicle, I found resolve. I remember thinking, "This is it," and I was ok with that. But then, once I realized I had survived, I was not happy or sad. In fact, I was just in a lot of pain. The idea of death had not scared me. But after hitting the other car, death was the furthest thing from my mind. I was ready to walk it off and get on with my weekend!

Fear of death is one thing, but allowing fear to control you is quite another. If we know what to expect, we can manage the symptoms of our fear and not allow it to immobilize us. Especially if it keeps us from sharing the good news with the people we meet along our journey.

The Struggle

"We are free to struggle,
We are not struggling to be free."

—Mike Donehey, Jeff Owen, Jason Jamison,
Ruben Juarez, Brendon Shirley
Tenth Avenue North, The Struggle (2012)

I sat on the edge of my bed and adjusted my slide board to scoot into my wheelchair. My mind was spinning. The realization that God had not only protected me but had spared me was fresh on my mind. My life was spared. I was only sitting there because God had spared my life. I was dumbfounded. Why?

I thought of all the prayer lists in our church bulletins over the years. The vast majority of prayer requests were for people who needed healing, and I was very aware of this. I thought back to the innumerable times, as a pastor or church leader, when I finished reviewing a prayer list during announcement time. It was then my responsibility to lead the congregation in prayer. Because the list was so long, I would often generalize "all those who need your healing" in a blanket prayer for those individuals. These were genuine prayers for God's intervention, but the list was always so long.

I remember praying for one of the elderly ladies in our church when I was a kid. For what seemed like many years, her name was on the top of the list. I don't remember ever meeting this person, but I remember praying for her to be healed. But she never was. She eventually died. This happened over and over again.

Survivor's remorse is where someone survives an incident and then feels guilty that they survived while others did not. This was different. I didn't feel guilty. It was more like confusion.

I had started scooting onto my wheelchair. I paused and prayed in my head, "Why? God, why did you spare me and not all these other people we prayed for?"

I wasn't struggling with my faith or doubting the power of prayer. I was just very confused. We had prayer for what I thought of as much more 'deserving' people that were not spared. Elderly folks, people suffering from awful illnesses, strong Christians, even children! There was a pastor I knew who had been faithful to God his whole life, had children who were raised in the truth, and had a very effective ministry. We prayed for him too, but he didn't make it.

There were many people who proclaimed, "God's not through with you yet. Better find out what he wants you to do!" or something very similar. This added to my confusion rather than clearing things up, because I was constantly asking God, "Why? Do you have a job for me, God?"

Days turned to weeks, and no reply came. I am not sure exactly what I was expecting. A lightning bolt, a burning bush, an email detailing an exact plan for me to follow—I don't know. I expected something though! I have always been a huge proponent of prayer! Over the years, I have had a number of friends who would spontaneously join together in prayer for any reason at the drop of a hat. Once I posted on social media that I would be working with a youth camp for a summer and asked for prayer warriors to cover the campers, staff, leaders, and volunteers in prayer. God came through—mightily! His presence was palpable that week!

By now, I made it from the edge of my bed to my wheelchair and I still had not heard from God. One of my favorite songwriters is Andrew Peterson. His songs have been an encouragement and challenge to me over the years and his song "The Silence of God" now rang so very true:

> *It's enough to drive a man crazy*
> *It'll break a man's faith*
> *It's enough to make him wonder*
> *if he's ever been sane*
> *When he's bleating for comfort*
> *from Thy staff and Thy rod*
> *And the heaven's only answer*
> *is the silence of God*

I was now hearing silence from God. Nothing. No direction. No big plan. Not even a "still small voice." I had heard all my life that God has a special plan for everyone. When I became a pastor, I thought I had answered the call. I thought I had accomplished the tasks he had given me. I was almost at my wit's end.

My favorite online Bible tool received a work-out over the next several days. I searched the Bible for every verse I could find on God's plan, his calling, or whatever I could find relevant to my situation. But, to borrow a phrase from Bono and the boys, I still hadn't found what I was looking for. I did not know why God had spared my life.

I have reached out to many people over the years for spiritual advice. Granted, I did not always take the advice I had solicited, but that may need to be saved for another book! This time I was desperately seeking guidance. I made a few calls and asked for help. The same answer resounded from everyone I talked to. "Seek God."

I had been seeking God, hadn't I? I was praying and reading the Bible. What was I missing? I started listing things out in my head. Family, money, the church, the lost, motorcycle safety. I didn't know where to turn, how to pray, or what to look up in the Bible any more. I was at a loss, with no answers.

Lesson Learned

"Well, sometimes my life
just don't make sense at all.
When the mountains look so big
And my faith just seems so small.
Hold me Jesus 'cause I'm shaking like a leaf.
You have been King of my glory.
Won't you be my Prince of Peace."
—Rich Mullins, Hold me Jesus

This must be the chapter for music quotes which is interesting because it falls in the chapter called The Struggle. Ephesians 5:19 tells us we can use songs to speak to each other. The context of this verse is talking about living by the Spirit and light. The chapter opens with the phrase, "Imitate God, therefore, in everything you do because you are his children." (Ephesians 5:1 NLT). So, I think it is fitting to use songs to speak to each other. Especially when working through struggles.

One struggle I think is largely overlooked in today's church is this question: "What do we do about God's calling?" I grew up in the church. All my life I heard we are supposed to seek God's will—we have to follow his plan for our lives. And everyone has a specific plan.

James 4:15 (ESV) was used to establish a precedent for every decision we made, "Instead you ought to say, 'If the Lord wills, we will live and do this or that.'" I don't know if I am the only one who feels this way, but hearing this verse used this way did not bring me comfort. If anything, it brought stress and anxiety! Not only did I have the responsibility of making decisions, they had to be the 'right' decisions or I might move outside of God's will. Wow!

We all face life-changing decisions. As a teen, it is a choice in sports, work, and what college to attend. As an adult, we decide on marriage, kids, career, etc. In all of these major life events, we place the stress on people to make sure it is within God's will. This is not only stressful, but it can cause doubt and worry. Is this God's will? How do I know?

One time, when I was much younger, I remember being paralyzed trying to decide if I should buy a particular CD (the music kind, if you know what that is). You might think it sounds ridiculous, but it had been pounded into my head that a Christian had to seek God's guidance on everything. In the church, we often tell people they need to seek God, but then we don't tell them how.

Now, don't get me wrong. I wholeheartedly believe we need to seek God and his will. However, the North American church has been fairly silent on how to do this or what God's 'will' even looks like. I have seen people who refused to date anyone for fear the would-be date might not be 'the one.' I have watched people suffer at dead-end jobs because God never 'called them away' from it. Churches are filled with people who sit in an audience week after week, waiting to understand God's will, when all they really want is to have God be active in their lives.

When we tell people God has a specific plan for them but then do not show them how to find out what that plan is, we can do damage to their faith. If they are waiting around to hear from God and they never do, they can start to doubt God's existence or think they just don't have enough faith.

I was sitting in my deer stand during hunting season several years ago and I got to thinking about what I was doing. I was sitting in one spot, stationary, looking around and hoping a deer would show up. I actually called it "hunting" too. The word itself demands movement. How can I call it hunting when I am not moving? I was just sitting...and waiting.

Sometimes it feels like this is how we teach people to find God's will. If you sit there long enough and are patient, then God will eventually show up! People imagine God's will as some idealistic imagery—an enigma no one knows how to find.

So what do we do for those of us who struggle to find "God's will?" The first thing we need to do is to define the term 'God's will' before we even attempt to tackle helping someone find it. Let's start with scope. I was taught that God's will governs everything in our lives, from the beginning to the end. A volunteer teacher for our teen class drew a timeline to help illustrate the point. The teacher then drew branches off of the timeline. Keep in mind this was circa 1988, not long after the first Back to the Future movie came out.

The chart the teacher drew looked strangely similar to Doc's chart as he was explaining the alternate timelines. In other words, I learned every time we make a choice, we are deciding between our own will and God's will. And if we choose our will we move onto one of the "alternate timelines" which changes our future. And, not unlike our hero, Marty McFly, we had to get back to 'God's future'—the real timeline he wanted us to be in our whole lives. Confused? We were too!

Granted, this was creative. But I did not learn that we ought to be seeking God's will. I learned every choice I make could land me in a future where Biff ran everything and crime and drugs were rampant! I learned to fear making choices. The scope of God's will, in my adolescent mind, not only ran from before I was born until after I died, but it included every single decision I made. Additionally, it would be compounded if I chose my will over God's will multiple times in a row—including purchasing that Metallica CD. Incidentally, it was the Black Album, so the decision should have been obvious.

My Bible tells me God doesn't want anyone to perish, but all would come to repentance (2 Peter 3:10). So, in that regard, yes, he has a plan for us. But here is where we often allow an over-spiritualized concept of God's will to cloud our vision. We need to consider God's will in our decision-making. But, I have found that if we change the word "will" to "desire" we can get a better understanding. God desires that we understand him and get to know him so we know the things that will please him.

How do you please your spouse? Was it by waiting for them to tell you what to do? How about pleasing your parents? I mastered this one! I followed my parents' will all the time. Waiting patiently, I would sit there and listen, doing absolutely nothing until I was told exactly what to do! I wouldn't do anything without specific and explicit direction. To clarify: I didn't clean my room, take out the trash, do dishes, or anything else unless my mom or dad told me to do it. My choices were always dictated by what my parents told me to do. And I know how much this brought them pleasure! Right?

Ok, maybe I hadn't figured it out. But I hope you see how this compares directly with "looking" for God's will. There was a time I did not know what my parents' will was. During those years I was mostly crying, eating, sleeping, or getting my diapers changed. As I started crawling, and then walking, I started to get a better idea of what my boundaries were. Eventually, I learned to communicate with my parents. They had been speaking to me this whole time, and I didn't really understand what was going on. But once I figured out how to talk back to them (wait, that came out wrong)...respond to them, it opened a whole new world (talking back did too, but that will need its own book).

God's will is not that we understand a direct path to the end of our life. It is that we live for him and try to please him in our decisions. Yes, we will choose the wrong thing from time to time. We will distance ourselves from Him. However, getting to know him and the things which please him will allow us to return to him. James 4:8 tells us, "Draw near to God and he will draw near to you." But then it describes the process on how to draw near to him, "Wash your hands, you sinner, and purify your hearts, you double minded."

This is the process of repenting—or, perhaps a better description is to change the way you think. Remember Jesus in the sermon on the mount? He said several times, "You have heard... But I tell you..." Here is the law, but here is the heart behind the law. Change the way you think about obedience. Anyone can decide not to murder someone and follow through with that determination with relatively easy success. But what about hating them? Jesus wants us to change the way we think about obedience. It is no longer a legalistic adherence to a law system like it was under the Old Covenant. The new covenant makes us seek God to understand the things which make him happy. He doesn't want us to sit there waiting to be told what to do.

Now, don't get me wrong, this does not make following Jesus any easier, and we still have to think things through. But understanding how we do it will help. Romans 12:2 (NLT) says, "Do not copy the behavior and customs of this world but allow God to transform you into a new person by changing the way you think. Then you will learn to know God's will for you, which is good and pleasing and perfect." This process of allowing God to transform us is echoed all over in the New Testament. God wants to make us new, restore us, mold us into his image, and clothe us with his likeness to the point that when people look at us they are not seeing us, but seeing God.

You know those elderly couples who start looking like each other. The ones who are perfectly happy sitting on a bench together holding hands. It wasn't easy for them to get there. There were fights and arguments, disagreements and misunderstandings. But they got to where they are because somewhere along the line they decided to look for the things they knew would bring their mate happiness.

That is what our heavenly father wants; children who do the things they know will make him happy, and avoid the things that make him sad. It is all any parent wants, really. Do you want to know God's will for your life? Love the things he loves, hate the things he hates. Yes, God desires obedience, but not out of force or obligation. He is the designer of free-will. He created humans to be capable of choosing to love him.

We need to make choices in this life, but God leaves those largely up to us. Does he guide us? Sure he does, much like a parent helping their child make a choice. And, much like a parent, sometimes God makes the choice for us. I have had many opportunities fall through that I really wanted to do, but God "closed the door" on me and said "No." This does not detract from what I said earlier about not being chess pieces God manipulates and forces into a cosmic ultimate agenda. I picture a toddler learning to walk—arms stretch to the max, grasping firmly on a parent's index fingers. Sometimes the parent lets go with one finger. Other times the parent grabs the child's wrists to keep them from falling over. And, of course, there are the occasions when the parent sweeps the child up in their arms and holds them tightly. Eventually, the child is walking and running around on its own with no support except for the gleaming faces of their parents approvingly cheering them on. Then the child stumbles, trips, and falls! A comforting embrace is all it takes for the child to be off and running again, maybe with a warning this time.

We have support, comfort, and guidance from a God who even notices when a sparrow falls to the ground. He is there for us even when he is silent. His silence is not disapproval, abandonment, or evidence that he does not exist. It is an opportunity to grow in faith. Like the father in Mark 9:24 (NIV), we can cry out to God, "I do believe; help me overcome my unbelief."

I did not get a direct answer from God right away. But as I cried out to him, sought Godly counsel, and searched his scriptures, his Spirit comforted me. I realized I already knew what his will was. I knew he wanted me to rely on him. I came before him, literally broken apart, and he ministered to my needs. This does not mean he gave me what I wanted, but he helped me with what I needed. I wanted answers, and he gave me healing for my brokenness.

Chapter 8 - The Struggle

The Body

*"The human body has many parts,
but the many parts make up one whole body.
So it is with the body of Christ."*
—1 Corinthians 12:12 (NLT)

The human body is an incredible masterpiece. It is not just bones and flesh, but a complex system that works together in perfect harmony. Well, at least it is designed to work together in perfect harmony. But when part of it is injured or stops working the way it is supposed to, it throws off the balance of the whole body. The good news, however, is that the body is also capable of healing.

As I write this, it has been just over seven months since my accident. Though I am not completely healed, my body is functioning and working toward recovery. My doctor told me I may never get fully back to where I was before, but I am certainly seeing improvements. I am focusing on strength exercises, stretching, and endurance. After sitting in a wheelchair for three months and not getting any exercise, I lost a lot of muscle mass in my larger muscle groups as well as adding weight to my upper body.

The first time I stood up after the accident was such a surreal experience. I will never forget it. It took a lot of effort to get up and every movement felt unnatural. I only took a couple steps to turn from my wheelchair to the vehicle. I felt steady, but it also felt like I should not be able to stand. My emotions played into the experience as well as the physics of my body acting in ways it had not acted in months.

My grin had to be one of the biggest I have ever had as I turned and stepped into the vehicle. At that moment, I had no idea how many difficulties I would have to face during the next three months. Right then, I felt like a new person. I felt like I had conquered the world. I was finally free.

Then I went to physical therapy. Now keep in mind, I have always been a fairly tough guy. I worked in masonry for fifteen years, so I was always fairly strong with a lot of drive. The therapy sessions were a challenge, but I knew I had what it took to push through the pain and regain my strength and range of motion. At least that is what my mind told my body, and for the most part, things did work that way—at least to begin with.

The therapy went just fine, and all the exercises were tolerable. My therapist was impressed with my ability to complete his whole regimen the first time through. I was determined to not let this part slow me down. I may have overdone it a few times during some of my sessions just to prove I could keep up with the stretches and routines prescribed.

I even got a gym membership and started doing some strength training. This is where things started to get real. Little did I know just how much strength I had lost in my legs. I did all the exercises and all the stretches, but I was not seeing results. I started taking protein supplements and added aerobic exercise but still did not see any results.

I would get stiff in all my joints from sitting or standing for any amount of time. My hips were in constant pain. I would get out of breath after doing the simplest of chores like loading the dishwasher or folding clothes. And worst of all—I could not jump! I used to be an amazing jumper. I could jump high and had decent hang-time for a chubby short guy! But now, I can barely get both feet off the ground!

I found out the lack of strength in my larger muscle groups in my legs had caused my smaller muscle groups, like my hip-flexors, to be overworked. My hips would almost burn with sharp pains and cause discomfort in absolutely every activity. The hip flexors were not made to carry the weight of my body, especially not my new weight! They were exhausted and let the rest of my body know they could not keep up.

I could walk and stand, but even that would get painful after short periods of time. I thought I just needed to work harder. Push through my exercises. Build muscle faster! Well, the body can only build muscle so fast. I was relying on the smaller muscles to do the work for the larger muscles and not building any of the muscles that needed to be built.

It took me a while to realize there was no quick fix. I just had to stick to it and do the hard work of building strength. I had to adjust my program to fit the demands of my body rather than just push through the pain and think I was getting stronger. In reality, I was only adding stress and strain to already stressed and strained muscles.

Sometimes doing more is not the best answer. I was doing more at the gym, but it was just making things worse. Instead of doing more, I needed to change the way I was doing things to help the parts of my body that needed help, and rest the parts that needed rest. Strengthen the parts that needed strengthened. I needed to allow the healing process to complete before pushing through into a more intense routine.

Lesson Learned

"The human body has many parts,
but the many parts make up one whole body.
So it is with the body of Christ."
—1 Corinthians 12:12 (NLT)

The profoundness of these words was clear to me prior to my accident. Since then, however, this entire chapter in 1 Corinthians has come alive to me. Paul's comparison of the human body and the body of Christ has blown my mind. What should have been so obvious has now been manifested in *my* body! This allowed me to reconsider the hurtful experiences, in-fighting, struggles, and conflicts I have observed and experienced within the body of Christ.

From the moment my motorcycle hit the other vehicle, I knew something was wrong, but couldn't pinpoint the problem. This happens all the time in churches. You can just tell there is something off, but you cannot articulate what the actual problem is. There is pain, but it is not exactly specific, so you can't tell what needs to be done about it.

When a church gets to this point there are several responses, at least from my experience. The first, and unfortunately, most common, is to ignore the pain and hope it eventually goes away. Sometimes it does go away.

Second, we attempt to self-diagnose. This can lead to figuring out the problem, but often does not. Instead, there are hushed meetings, closed doors, shifts in leadership, or even people that end up cut off from the rest of the body—for better or worse—in an attempt to control the damage.

Third, someone realizes they caused the problems (or it is pointed out to them in a kind and loving way) and restoration and healing takes place and the body can move on. Again, from my experience, this is rare and is often overlooked because it does not draw mass amounts of attention due to a quick resolution.

Fourth, we realize the problem is bigger than we can deal with and call in the experts. This has happened to me on several occasions. We had consultants brought in, authorities on conflict resolution, experts, and specialists, to try to fix the damage that has been inflicted upon the body.

Now, the responses to these experts can follow the same line as we faced above. They can be ignored, they can be overridden in favor of a self-diagnosis, or they can lead to healing. The latter is often the hardest result and can be the most painful. This route will often involve therapies, treatments, and even exercises to work through hurt and pain, but can ultimately lead to healing if they are followed properly.

Just like the physical therapy and exercises I endured, they can be difficult and require consistency and determination. You have to be willing to endure and push through each step of the process. And you can't rush it or skip a few uncomfortable steps! You have to follow the plan.

I have seen these healing processes start many times, and I am sure they began with good intentions from all parties involved. But somewhere during the process one part of the body wanted to rush ahead while another seemed to lag behind. Or, it just hurt too bad so the whole process was abandoned. Either way, just like Paul said to the church in Corinth, "If one part suffers, all the parts suffer with it." —1 Corinthians 12:26a (NLT).

Then there are the times when I have seen restoration actually take place. The entire process endured, the plan followed, the pain and struggles worked through, and actual healing started to take place. This is an extremely vulnerable place to be, because it may give a false sense of healing. Or the body may think it is healed fully and try to stand, walk, or run too soon and end up re-injuring the same part that was hurt to begin with. The healing has to be complete before taking on the full force of whatever activity hurt it to begin with.

But what about all the different types of injuries a body can suffer? Does this same process apply to all of them? Well, not necessarily—but to some extent, yes. I hope that was as ambiguous as I intended it to be. See, there are so many moving parts in a body that not every injury will be treated exactly the same.

Consider a headache, for instance. Sometimes headaches can be endured until they go away. Sometimes headaches are indicative of brain tumors. Two very different types of problems, and, of course, very different kinds of treatments. Muscle pain vs broken bones; diseased kidneys vs gastric pains; twisted ligaments vs skin rashes. This list could go on and on. Some can be medicated while others may need specialized care. The process of evaluation might look very similar in each case, but the way the problems are treated—the exercise plan, therapy, or medicines—will vary greatly!

I want to speak to one specific issue I had during my healing experience that is a very prevalent struggle in churches I have either observed or been a part of. I had gotten very comfortable with the leg press machine and decided to push harder than normal. When I got off the machine, there was an extremely sharp pain in my hip. I was sure I had torn something or re-injured the break. I discovered later I had not yet developed enough muscle in my thighs and hamstrings to push that hard. Despite my regular workouts, I had lost so much mass from sitting that I still had a long way to go. I had stressed the small hip flexors, which typically only assist movement of the legs. They were never intended to carry the load of the whole body, let alone additional weights from the leg-press machine.

Do you know the church has larger "muscle groups" that are intended to carry the weight of the body, as well as support it and propel it forward? These groups often get over-worked, tired, burned out, or even atrophied from lack of use. Then the smaller "muscle groups" which were never intended to do all the work try to step up. This can work for a short time, until those muscles burn out or become exhausted. They were designed to assist, and now they are taking on far more weight and control than they are able to handle. This can be catastrophic and lead to even greater injuries.

To put it bluntly, leaders, pastors, elders, or teachers are vulnerable to burn-out, injury, pain, and even atrophy. When this happens, the smaller groups such as volunteers, ladies' prayer circles, Sunday School committees, or even the teens/children in the church end up pulling the weight of the whole body. The leaders they once turned to for support have stopped working. These other groups feel the need to push on even though they are not equipped for the challenge. Then they start to think it is now up to them to be the spiritual leaders. This may work for a short time, but since they were not equipped for it, they burn out quickly or fail to pull the whole weight and end up injuring themselves or others around them. This, of course, has a cascading effect that has the potential to incapacitate an entire body.

In these situations, the whole body has to unite in an attempt to restore the proper functions to the whole body before it tries to push forward. This often requires the use of an outside entity—a specialist or expert—to set the body on a path of healing before it will ever be ready to move again. This can often be a painful process. But it has to be done in order to restore the proper motions the body requires to move forward.

In some extreme circumstances, a body can die from its wounds. But guess what? As followers of a risen savior, we know death is not the end! We know there is hope for resurrection—for revival! I once heard a speaker say, "You cannot plan a revival." He elaborated that revival implies death. You have to admit death before revival can happen. He also pointed out Jesus Christ was raised from the dead by the power of the Spirit of God (Romans 8:11). In the same way, the Spirit can bring revival to the Body of Christ—the church. We must rely on the Spirit of the living God to bring revival to a dead church. That takes humility, submission, obedience, unity, brokenness, and love. This is not an exhaustive list, of course, but it can be exhausting to follow! However, if we stick to the plan, follow the process, and let God lead, we can see exactly what He is capable of. And my Bible tells me it will be more than I can ask for or even imagine!

Isaiah 35:3-6a says:

> *Strengthen the weak hands, and*
> *make firm the feeble knees. Say to*
> *those who have an anxious heart, "Be*
> *strong; fear not! Behold, your God*

will come with vengeance, with the
recompense of God. He will come and
save you." Then the eyes of the blind
shall be opened, and the ears of the
deaf unstopped; then shall the lame
man leap like a deer, and the tongue
of the mute sing for joy.

God created our bodies. He made us with parts that deteriorate, wear-out, break, and even die. But he planned for that too! He included a way for new life to be breathed into the dead; for restoration and healing to reanimate a beaten and broken body. We were created in a corruptible body, but we can see from the beginning of God's word to the end, we serve a God of restoration. He can restore health and strength, he can give sight to the blind, hearing to the deaf, and cause the lame to walk. All these miracles were performed so we can see the mighty power of our God and glorify him in humble adoration. I believe it was also to help us recognize the restorative nature of our God. This motivates us to reflect his image and be restorative people.

Paul tells us all these different parts in the body are going to function in different ways, even when we are all gathered together. In 1 Corinthians 14:26 (NIV) he concluded, "...Everything must be done so that the church may be built up." Another translation of this same verse uses the word "edify." This single word includes uplifting, encouraging, instructing, improving, enlightening, and informing!

My body was broken to the point it could not carry out its every-day functions. I believe the church can get to the same point. It can be injured to the point where the members cannot carry out what God called the church to do. It is no wonder we see an unprecedented number of churches close their doors in North America. It is estimated around 4,000 churches close every year in this country. That is incredible. These churches would not be closing if they were functioning the way they ought to be functioning.

This leads to an even greater problem. All these churches who are closing down are not individual smaller separate bodies of Christ. They are part of the body. And, if one part suffers, the whole body suffers with it! Paul says we are all members of one body. 1 Peter 2:5 says we are living stones that all build together a spiritual temple. It is no wonder there is so much in scripture instructing us to work on building up the church.

Once we realize we are broken and need healing, we can take the necessary steps toward healing. Until then, we will not find the healing our creator desires for his body.

Broken

It has now been over a year since my accident. My physical body has its ups and downs. I am getting used to the idea of my physical limitations. Not everything is 'butterflies and rainbows' and these limitations can certainly wreak havoc on my emotions. I have maintained a positive outlook, but I have also collapsed on my bed and bawled like a baby.

These varying degrees of responses to my current situation are often confusing. It has been a challenge, but taking it one day at a time has become normal. One day I am full of energy and want to attack all the little projects around the house I have been neglecting. Then the next day I am paralyzed, either physically from overdoing it, or emotionally from overthinking it.

I have always been a dreamer—a big-picture kind of guy. I like to visualize the future in whatever way my imagination carries it. When I look at my current situation, it is more difficult to visualize what the future might look like. Am I ever going to get back to 'normal' or is this my 'new normal?' I have talked to others who have endured similar accidents and they are still dealing with aches and pains several years later.

You have probably heard of people who can predict the weather because they can "feel it" in their bones. Apparently, this is a real thing. My doctor told me it has to do with changes in atmospheric pressure that effects the broken bones and allows some to 'feel' when the weather is changing. With the recent shift from summer to fall, I am connecting some of my phantom pains with the changes in weather. I can already picture myself in a rocking chair on the porch crooning about how "the rains be a-comin'. I can feel it in me bones!" (of course I am dressed like a pirate, eye-patch and all.)

I can understand the idea that this may be the extent of my healing and I will be 'broken' for the rest of my life. I can also recognize that I can do something about my broken state.

I was given very specific physical therapy to work on during the first several months of learning to walk again. The exercises were difficult—bearable, but difficult. I knew I had to keep up with them just like when I was doing in-patient therapy. Back then, I knew I had to do it so I could get out of the wheelchair and start walking again. Now I know I have to maintain my strength so I can still walk when I turn sixty.

I was going to the gym five to six days a week and following my therapist's regimen almost perfectly. I reached a point where I was feeling fine—I was comfortable with my progress. That became a very dangerous place for me and after a while I stopped exercising. Sure, I would do some stretches here and there if I got particularly stiff, but I basically just assumed the state of my body was as good as it is going to get, so I stopped trying so hard to improve it.

As you can imagine, this did not help my situation. I started declining again as the scar tissue began tightening. This directly impacted my mobility, but it happened so slowly over a period of what I thought was relaxing time but as it turned out, I had become lackadaisical.

I was faced with a choice. I could continue with the mindset that there was nothing I could do, or I could change my mindset. That is not an easy thing to do. It is much easier to—for lack of a better term—give up. I knew trying to change would be hard work and take a lot of time. I had to decide if it was worth it.

Eventually I was motivated enough, sometimes only by the growing pain in my hips, that I started exercising again. I realized I could not stay "relaxed" without losing all I had worked for. I knew I did not want that. As difficult as it was to change, I knew it would be better than hobbling through the rest of my life on hips that didn't work right. I knew what I had to do, so now, I just had to do it.

Lesson Learned

*"If the Lord shall break
your heart, consent to
have it broken."*
—C. H. Spurgeon

God is God, and I am not! Understanding this one fact is the first step in becoming broken before God. When we recognize the sovereignty of God it is the first step in putting ourself in our proper place. This is crucial, because when we believe ourselves to be sovereign, it puts God in second place.

Yes, there is a long way between putting yourself in second place and being broken before God, but we all have to start somewhere. For me, it was recognizing God has much more power and control than I have.

The next reasonable step is to elevate God above ourselves. This may seem obvious, but in today's culture, we are inundated with the idea that no one is more important than 'self.' It is easy to view my morals as higher than everyone else's morals. It is easy to think of myself as better than those around me. However, the Apostle Paul challenges us to think of others as "more significant than yourselves" (Philippians 2:3, ESV). This allows us to recognize we are not the ones on top—even in our social circles. When we view ourselves as the most important person in the room, it raises us above everyone else.

We need to understand humility. This does not mean we belittle ourselves or put ourselves down in public. That is not humility. C. S. Lewis was quoted as saying, "Humility is not thinking less of yourself, but thinking of yourself less." Humility allows us to point the spotlight at others rather than vying to be in it ourselves.

This is certainly a step toward brokenness, but it still leaves us whole – just slightly abased. I am not a proponent of thinking we all need to hit rock bottom in life to recognize our position before God, but hear me out on this one.

David was considered a man after God's own heart (1 Samuel 13:14; Acts 13:22, NIV). But look at what he went through. He was a murderer, an adulterer, and a liar. He was all-kinds of evil. David did terrible things—knowingly. He chose the wrong door, time after time, choice after choice. Even after God had lifted him to a powerful position, he continued to make terrible choices. So how in the world was he considered a man after God's own heart?!

Psalm 51:3 says, "For I know my transgressions, and my sin is ever before me" (ESV).

Psalm 8:4, "...what are mere mortals that you should think about them, human beings that you should care for them?"

2 Samuel 7:18b, "...Who am I, O Sovereign LORD, and what is my family, that you have brought me this far?"

Psalm 51:17, "My sacrifice, O God, is a broken spirit; a broken and contrite heart you, God, will not despise."

These are only a few examples of David recognizing his place before God. He understood his position was much lower than that of an almighty and sovereign God. He understood he was much lower of a being, and even in a position of subjugation to the only one who is supreme and exalted.

In recognizing where we stand before God, we admit our inability to control a situation. We admit that we are not in control, even if we attempt to put up some facade that we are. When we recognize where we are in comparison to God, we put ourselves in a humbled position. This helps us take a backseat and allows God to take control. It is always much better to put yourself in this position rather than being put there by someone else.

When we pretend to be the one in control, we are attempting to take to the position of God. We usurp control in an attempt to put on the appearance of being in control.

This may be a shock to some, but God will not share his throne. He is either in power, or he is not. This is the constant game we play in this life. We pretend to be in power for a time, but then, when our power seems to wane momentarily, we offer power back over to God for a moment. It is not as if we are not really in control, but we feel like we are on top of the world with everything going our way. The 'top' is a precarious place to be and we often fall from this great height. It may just be a small or momentary lapse for us, but then we are back on top, with no holds barred.

This is not submission to God. This is not brokenness. This is a power struggle. This is an attempt to take control and power from God. No, we would never say out loud that we are attempting to regain control, or usurp power; but our actions will always speak louder than our words.

Someone who is preying on the weakness of others is attempting to control. A person who is subjugating others is flexing their power in an attempt to show superiority. These are attempts to strengthen one's position over others, not to show that others are more important than themselves. This is a spirit which is in direct conflict with what God desires—a broken and contrite spirit (Psalm 51:17).

God is in control. I am not in control. God is sovereign and I am the subjugate. God is powerful and I am powerless. God is God and I am not. If only we can get this through our head, we can recognize, not only our brokenness before God, but our powerlessness to be in control.

When we recognize just how powerless we are, it helps us see how powerful God is. It helps us see he does not want to 'put us in our place' or humiliate us. He wants to help us. Psalm 34:18 says, "...the Lord is near to the brokenhearted and saves the crushed in spirit." (ESV) Psalm 147:3 says, "...he heals the brokenhearted and binds up their wounds." (NIV)

The Apostle Paul stated this another way. In 2 Corinthians 12:9, 10 he says this:

> *"But he said to me, 'My grace is sufficient for you, for my power is made perfect in weakness.' Therefore I will boast all the more gladly about my weaknesses, so that Christ's power may rest on me. That is why, for Christ's sake, I delight in weaknesses, in insults, in hardships, in persecutions, in difficulties. For when I am weak, then I am strong."*

Jesus gave us an example of taking a lesser seat first at a banquet, because it would be a lot better if the host invited you to a more honored seat than if he had to ask you to move to a lesser seat. Have you ever accidentally sat in a 'reserved' seat and been asked to move? It is humiliating. Knowing our position from the beginning will save us from this embarrassment.

"The measure of intelligence is the ability to change."
— *Albert Einstein*

The ability to change is crucial in becoming broken before God. We cannot simply confess our sins or be open about being sinful beings. We must change. We must allow God's Spirit to work in us to change our mindset.

I am sure we have all heard the explanation of repenting as 'turning around.' I had a teacher in my youth group when I was only a teenager who was attempting to make this point. After describing 'repentance' as turning around, he placed a garbage can on the floor and told me to walk over to the garbage can and 'repent.' I walked up to the garbage can and picked it up, turned it around, and placed it back on the floor. The teacher said, "Thank you. But I wanted you to turn around, not the garbage can."

I look back now, and I can understand the point the teacher was trying to make. Truth be told, I probably understood it back then also, but could not help but point out the ambiguity or resist the urge to make the whole class laugh. However, this simplistic look at repentance may not be the best example. It does demonstrate a physical turning going from one direction, then heading back the other way. Presumably, we are walking away from God, then we repent and start walking toward God.

I want to attempt a deeper explanation. Repentance does indeed imply change. However—much more than a change of direction—it requires a change of mind. It requires us to change the way we think about the situation. Yet it goes so much further than merely admitting we are wrong; though that is part of the process. It must include remorse as well. Even further, it cannot just be sorrow that your wrong was exposed, but genuine desire to make things right again. This is where the change of mind takes root and grows into true repentance.

This comes full circle when we shift our focus from ourselves back to God. If our goal is to bear the image of God, but our actions miss the mark, we call it sin. Repentance is not only turning our hearts and minds back toward God, but also shifting our lives back into line with him to begin reflecting him. As the Apostle Paul said in Galatians 2:20b (NLT), "It is no longer I who lives, but Christ lives in me."

Becoming broken before God is what allows us to fully repent and begin shining his light through our lives. It is falling on our face before our God and allowing him to pick up the pieces and put them back together. He created us in his image, and he can re-create us when we are broken. The difficult part is allowing him to complete his work. We can become comfortable in our brokenness and come to believe that we cannot recover. But God's desire is to heal and mend us back into his image.

In 2 Corinthians 4:5-7 (NLT), Paul talks about this shining light we are reflecting. He says this:

> *"For what we proclaim is not ourselves, but Jesus Christ as Lord, with ourselves as your servants for Jesus' sake. For God, who said, "Let light shine out of darkness," has shone in our hearts to give the light of the knowledge of the glory of God in the face of Jesus Christ. But we have this treasure in jars of clay, to show that the surpassing power belongs to God and not to us."*

He compares us to fragile clay jars. Our choices can certainly damage this vessel that allows us to carry God's message. But even if we smash that jar to bits, God can pick up the pieces and rework his masterpiece, without fault or defect, perfectly reflecting his image again, as it was originally intended.

Faithfulness

*"But you must remain faithful to the things
you have been taught. You know they are true,
for you know you can trust
those who taught you.
You have been taught the
holy Scriptures from childhood,
and they have given you
the wisdom to receive the salvation that comes
by trusting in Christ Jesus."
—2 Timothy 3:14, 15 (NLT)*

This is the final chapter. My story is done. After what happened to me, I should not be here. However, since I am, I am striving to live out what Paul said in Galatians 2:20 (ESV), "It is no longer I who live, but Christ who lives in me." I have no doubt God not only protected me, but spared my life. This is the perfect opportunity for me to realize just how much I had been living for myself up to this point even though I told everyone I was living for God. It helped me realize what I say I believe and what I actually believe can be two very different things. What I say I believe can be faked while what I actually believe will be demonstrated in my every-day choices!

I had lived what I thought to be a "faithful" life. What made me think I was being faithful? Well, I call myself a Christian and I believe what the Bible says is true. I am generally honest with people. I am generous with my money as well as being financially responsible, well, for the most part anyway. I attend church, at least when I don't have prior obligations that may keep me from attending. I also participated in a public display of my faith by being baptized—twice! I was a preacher, for goodness' sake. Obviously, this is what a faithful Christian looks like...Right? On top of all this, all the other "faithful Christians" around me lived very similar lives.

As I have already said, I have never heard an audible voice from God. But after several weeks of calling out to him and asking him to tell me why he spared me, I had one resounding thought come back to me—be faithful. "But...I have been faithful," I thought. I was doing everything God required, wasn't I? I kept my honor, I admitted my faults, I talked about God all the time. Wasn't this faithfulness?

As these thoughts bounced around in my head, confusion set in. Why would God spare me to "be faithful?" I had been faithful. I was sure of it. I had no choice at this point but to try to figure out what God meant.

I always thought being faithful to God meant faithfully attending church, faithfully reading my Bible even when I didn't feel like it, faithfully giving money to the church, and faithfully avoiding sinful activities. This was what I considered to be the basic duties of all Christians. Little did I realize we were never called to fulfill basic duties. Jesus taught a parable about that. He told about a man who had a servant working in the field. When all the work was done for the day, the man would not thank his servant for performing basic duties. Jesus ended his thought with this, "So you also, when you have done everything you were told to do, should say, 'We are unworthy servants; we have only done our duty." —Luke 17:10 (NIV).

Faithfulness is a theme mentioned often enough in scripture that we ought to pay attention to it. Paul encouraged Timothy to "Work at telling others the Good News, and fully carry out the ministry God has given you." —2 Timothy 4:5b (NLT).

An example from Jesus is recorded in John 4:34 (NLT), "My nourishment comes from doing the will of God, who sent me, and from finishing his work."

How about Acts 20:24 (BSB), "I consider my life of no value to me, if only I may finish my course and complete the ministry I have received from the Lord Jesus—the ministry of testifying to the good news of God's grace."

So, it would seem faithfulness to God's work and sharing his good news is a pretty big deal. My struggle was in thinking I was already faithful to God. Hadn't I fought the good fight, finished the race, and kept the faith? Wasn't I just biding my time until I got my crown of righteousness? Wasn't I in a long line of other Christians just waiting for the pearly gates to fling open to welcome me home?

This question caused me to ponder my life choices. I knew God was there. I knew he was my maker and creator—the sustainer of life! I proclaimed to people around me, "I am following Jesus with my life." That is when I realized the implication of the word 'follow.' It requires movement! When Jesus first called his disciples, he used this phrase, "Follow me."

The results were recorded in the gospels of Matthew, Mark, and Luke; they left their nets/boats and followed him. There was movement. There was sacrifice. They gave something up and followed Jesus.

When I was self-evaluating, however biased I may have been, I was recognizing movement. I had to move from my couch to get to church, right? I had to move to my bookshelf to pick up my Bible to read it. I had to move my hand to my wallet to give money. With all of these qualifiers, I could justify that I was moving, and therefore, must have been actually following Jesus. I was able to convince myself of this even more by pointing out some other unmistakable markers indicative of a follower of Jesus. Mostly, I did not look like all of those people out there who were obviously *not* following him. They didn't even attend church! Which means they probably didn't even pray or read their Bibles. I thank God I am not like those cheaters, sinners, adulterers, and tax collectors...

Oh, wait a minute. I think Jesus talked about someone who said something very similar. He said people who pray like this, exalting themselves, will be humbled! All the things I did in the name of 'following Jesus' were done to make sure the people around me could see what I was doing. I was more interested in making it look like I was following Jesus than I was in following him!

That is when I started thinking about what I knew God wanted from his followers. John 14:15 (NIV) quotes Jesus saying, "If you love me, keep my commands." This verse seems to have been dropped right in the middle of Jesus trying to help his disciples understand his true identity. Keep in mind that these were Jewish men who were taught to follow the Law of Moses. So, for Jesus to say, 'keep my commands' would have been a challenge to the law system of the Jewish teaching. Think back to Jesus's Sermon on the Mount. He took a Law, or command, and then contrasted it with the heart of the matter. You have heard...But I tell you...

We have to understand Jesus was not implementing a new law system. He was not saying his new laws would override the previous laws. We know this because Jesus rebuked the religious leaders of his time for doing exactly that. The religious leaders had built their own set of laws around God's laws. Then they were enforcing their laws to keep people from breaking God's laws. Jesus called them out on it and told them they were crushing people with unbearable religious demands (Luke 11:46).

In his Sermon on the Mount, Jesus was drilling down to the heart of the law. He was doing the same thing when he told the expert in the law the greatest command was to love God and love others. Now, I have heard people suggest Jesus was simply summarizing the Ten Commandments with this new commandment. This is how I have heard it explained: if you love God you will not break laws 1-4, and if you love others, you will not break laws 5-10. But what Jesus was doing was the exact opposite of this. He was saying the reason we don't kill people is because we love them. The reason we don't worship other gods is because we love the one true God.

In any culture on this globe, if you started killing people and stealing their belongings, your actions would certainly be looked down upon. There is nothing inherently Christian about this. When we over spiritualize the Law of Moses and state that our love for others still needs to satisfy the demands of the Law, we do not realize the implications. This demonstrates an ignorance of what the Law did. The Law condemned. It led to sin and death. It did not offer justification, forgiveness, grace, or even righteousness before God. It was inadequate because it could not bring life. That is why Jesus came, so he could fulfill the just requirements of the law. We will never be able to do that. Even if we could, the law would still not be able to justify us before God.

I have heard people who call themselves Christian say, "I have to love you, but that doesn't mean I have to like you." What they have done here is reverted to a law system. They believe love is something they are forced to do. It is a command that must be obeyed. It is the Law! But love doesn't work that way. This statement of being forced to love someone you dislike undermines the concept of grace and free will. It would be the same as saying you will love someone but hate every minute of it. Dear Reader, that is not love.

When Jesus gave the new command in John 13, he was not establishing a new law system. He was demonstrating that the law could force action, but love was a choice. He was saying I want you to obey me, not out of obligation and fear, but because you want to. It is in the context of this verse where Jesus is trying to get his followers to understand that he is going away and the Holy Spirit would come upon them. This would usher in a new covenant. One based on grace that included free-will. Specifically, Jesus was trying to get his disciple to realize the Holy Spirit would be sent to help them in the choices they were going to face.

The Apostle Paul understood this. He goes so far as to say the law only leads to death! 2 Corinthians 3:7-9 (NLT) demonstrates his thoughts:

The old way, with laws etched in stone, led to death, though it began with such glory that the people of Israel could not bear to look at Moses' face. For his face shone with the glory of God, even though the brightness was already fading away. Shouldn't we expect far greater glory under the new way, now that the Holy Spirit is giving life? If the old way, which brings condemnation, was glorious, how much more glorious is the new way, which makes us right with God!

Back to the topic of faithfulness. I said all this to circle back to my struggle with the idea of what it means to be faithful. I cannot stress enough that this does not refer to doubling our efforts on a rigorous path of unquestioning adherence to a set of laws. That was the old way. Faithfulness is the quality of remaining loyal or true to another. Think of it in regard to marriage. I remain faithful to my wife because of my devotion to her, not because I am obligated to. I love her and therefore want to please her with my faithfulness to her. This is not motivated because I dwell on all the negative outcomes that would result from unfaithfulness. I do not remain faithful because I am afraid of what will happen if I am unfaithful. In the same way, I do not hold my relationship with her over her head and demand her loyalty. I love my wife and I know she loves me!

There is a dichotomy of motivation between devotion and obligation. Jesus does not hold things over our head and force our actions through obligation. He, instead, requests our devotion. He desires us to choose to love him, not begrudgingly adhere to a set of rules because the alternative is eternal damnation in hell! That would be the cruelest religion on earth!

The gospel message is one of life and hope, not death and damnation. Now, don't get me wrong here. I am not saying that death and damnation, or hell, is not real. There certainly is an eternal afterlife for those who are not followers of Jesus as well as those who are. But, that ought not be the motivating factor. Granted, there are many who decided to follow Jesus out of fear, or even self-preservation, but as they mature in their understanding, they realize Jesus wants so much more for us than to live in fear.

My faithfulness to God is founded on love and will continue in the same vein. It is a loyalty that resulted from his love for me. His faithfulness to me led to my faithfulness to him. I love him because he first loved me (1 John 4:19). Just like I do not base my wife's devotion and faithfulness to me on how much she obeys my commands—God does not base our faithfulness to him based on obedience. Through his amazing grace, he remains faithful to us despite our disobedience.

Think of King David, whom the Bible refers to as a "man after God's own heart." Here is a man who had so much blood on his hands that God would not allow him to build the temple. He was manipulative, a liar, an extortionist, a murderer, and an adulterer. However, he was also broken before God! "A broken and contrite heart, O God, you will not despise!" (Psalm 51:17b, ESV). He knew he was unworthy. He was always aware of his sinfulness. He recognized his place before God.

David was faithful, not necessarily in obedience, but in his love for God. He stayed committed to God despite his human condition. He remained loyal and devoted to the God he loved regardless of how many times he fell short.

This is a testimony to every person who will decide to commit their life to God. We know everyone falls short of God's glory and we all sin. But we have to know our place before our Savior. We have to recognize it is only because of Jesus and his righteousness that we can be freed from our sins. Yes, our sins lead to death, but God's gift of grace leads to life! It is in God's grace that we can stand boldly before his throne.

Faithfulness is not simply following a set of rules, but remaining true to God even after we make the choice to not follow those rules. I mentioned Proverbs 3:6 back in chapter two. It says, "In all your ways acknowledge him and he will make straight your paths." That means *all* your ways, not just the good things you do. Not just when you are steadily obeying everything God commands, but even when you are not obedient. When you are turning away from God or toward him;

when you are at your lowest or your highest; when you are sick or well; in all your ways recognize the presence of God. He will set you back on the right path if you remain faithful to him.

Faithfulness is devotion and commitment. When I was questioning my purpose and heard God respond with a request for faithfulness something crystallized in my brain. My purpose in life is to bring glory and honor to my God through the things I do and say. It is to bring attention to him and what he has done. It is admitting when I fall short and turning to him to lift me up. It is making sure he gets the credit for accomplishments. It is showing his love to those around me. It is telling his story through my life. He must increase, but I must decrease (John 3:30).

I want to end with this encouragement from Paul to Timothy, in 2 Timothy 3:14-4:5:

> But you must remain faithful to the things you have been taught. You know they are true, for you know you can trust those who taught you. You have been taught the holy Scriptures from childhood, and they have given you the wisdom to receive the salvation that comes by trusting in Christ Jesus. All Scripture is inspired by God and is useful to teach us what is true and make us realize what is wrong in our lives. It corrects us when we are wrong and teaches us to do what is right. God uses it to prepare and equip his people to do every good work.
>
> I solemnly urge you in the presence of God and Christ Jesus, who will someday judge the living and the dead when he comes to set up his Kingdom: Preach the word of God. Be prepared, whether or not the time is favorable. Patiently correct, rebuke, and encourage your people with good teaching. For a time is coming when people will no longer listen to sound

and wholesome teaching. They will follow their own desires and will look for teachers who will tell them whatever their itching ears want to hear. They will reject the truth and chase after myths. But you should keep a clear mind in every situation. Don't be afraid of suffering for the Lord. Work at telling others the Good News, and fully carry out the ministry God has given you.

Afterward

It is easy to talk at length about something that needs to change and even feel convicted to actually do something about it. Unfortunately, we tend to keep things theoretical in our Christianity. The North American church likes to be challenged, but we fall short in the follow-through. I am guilty of it—being a hearer only and not a doer. I have often "known the good I ought to do, and do it not." (James 4:17) I have grown weary of being all talk, so I am including this portion of the book to give practical and applicable advice that pertains to each chapter of the book.

Below you will find actionable things you can put into place today to help you on your walk with Jesus. This is by no means exhaustive, nor is it a directive. They are simple suggestions I have found encouraging and challenging as I attempt to show God's love to others.

Chapter One: The Accident

The central focus of my life should not be me. If you want to develop a spiritual discipline of selflessness, you must start small. One practical thing you can do is repeat these words whenever you get offended or hurt by someone, 'You are more important than me."

This will solidify your RE-actions as telling more about your character than your actions. Avoiding conflict is impossible. How you respond to conflict will tell people your true feelings.

Another exercise is to take others into consideration when making major choices. How will my decisions affect those around me? Your choices will influence your family, friends, acquaintances, and even co-workers. Take their reactions into consideration when making choices. This is in no way promoting the idea that you need to stay in an unhealthy situation because you need to think of others as better than yourself. Jesus did not command anyone to be a doormat. If you are suffering abuse, find help and get out!

One last practical way to develop a biblical mindset in this area is to find ways to verbalize your worship to God. If you see something beautiful in nature (or anywhere else), say a verbal 'thank you' to the one who created it. When you recognize admirable qualities in another person, acknowledge the image of God this quality is reflecting; then praise God for displaying himself. As consistently as you think of it, give God the glory for anything which demonstrates his power. From natural beauty to creative works of art, from protection to provision, let God know you see his work.

Chapter Two: The Aftermath

I love the depiction of communication with God in the film, Fiddler on the Roof. Tevye will just start talking to God about any and everything. One of my favorite quotes is when he says to God in a matter-of-fact tone, "It may sound like I'm complaining, but I'm not. After all, with Your help, I'm starving to death." Whether Tevye was happy with God, disappointed in him, or even outright mad at him, he always kept the communication open.

Keep communication with God open. Do not fall prey to the 'formalities' of prayer. Talking to God is much more about the posture of our heart than our physical posture. But even when you feel distant from God, let him know you feel distant. When you feel close, tell him. Make it a practice to point out to yourself the times in a day you acknowledge the presence of God. Do it regularly. This will help you develop an open communication even when you don't feel like talking to God.

Remember, God is always present—whether you want him to be or not. He knows what is going on in our hearts, our heads, and behind closed doors. This is not a threat or a scare tactic. It is an acknowledgment of his presence. Whatever you are doing, know that God is there with you. He already knows about it. This will help you when you finally repent and decide to talk to him about your choices.

Be present with God. After all, he is present with you.

Chapter Three: The Injuries

Be honest with people. If they ask you how you are doing, don't lie. This does not mean you need to air out your dirty laundry with everyone all the time. But being honest allows others the opportunity to help. It also allows them the opportunity to be honest with you. This doesn't always work, but you'd be surprised how many people are just as tired of faking it as you are.

Tell people you are not sinless. Acknowledging this will benefit you and the ones you are with. It will lower your self-righteousness—which I believe we all possess to a certain extent. It opens you up to the idea that you are not perfect. This will be especially beneficial when you are around non-Christians. One of the biggest complaints non-Christians have with Christians is that we are a bunch of hypocrites. Acknowledging our faults, mistakes, and poor choices around non-Christians will show them you are not pretending to be perfect. This is even more meaningful when you apologize for the way you speak or act. In the same vein, forgive others when they apologize! This will free you from the hurt as well as relieve them from the guilt of their actions.

Finally, point to God's grace every time you recognize it. It is only by his grace that we can be saved. No matter how much we polish the outside of our cup, only he can clean the inside. Only through Jesus' example can you react to others as he did. You can only forgive because you have experienced forgiveness. You can only show grace because grace has been shown to you. You can only love because you have been loved!

Chapter Four: The Hospital

Find someone who has Godly characteristics you admire and ask them if you can spend more time with them. The idea of discipleship can only be accomplished in community. Do not isolate yourself in an attempt to protect yourself from getting hurt or hurting others. Instead, develop a Christian community with people who are demonstrating Christ-likeness.

Find people who care about your spiritual health. Be open with these people about your struggles. Vulnerability can be a blessing. We are not meant to struggle through this life alone. That is why we have the illustration of the church being like a family. We are all working together in this and for the common good.

Do not dwell on negativity. I know this should be obvious, but some of the obvious things ought to be pointed out more regularly. They can sometimes be overlooked because we think they should be obvious. We think avoiding negativity should go without saying, but we often bring up negativity to test the waters with people to see if they agree with you.

When these topics come up, call it out. Ask how it will bring glory and honor to God. Request that people don't gossip around you. Change the subject, or walk away, if necessary. Don't drag other people down for gossiping, and don't put yourself on a pedestal of self-righteousness. Humbly and kindly suggest that dwelling on negative topics or dragging people's name through the mud is not beneficial to anyone. If people are bad, then others will already know, you don't have to point it out in an attempt to show others how bad they are. People will know them by their actions.

Chapter Five: My Darkest Night

Pursue understanding from the Holy Spirit. Ask specifically that God search your heart and your anxious thoughts. Ask him to point out your offensive ways. Next, do this in the community. Be open to critical corrections. When you offer these types of corrections, do it in a way that you would want it done to you. Let people know you care about them and you can see areas where they may be self-blind. But only do this through humility, kindness, and gentleness. And, always, always, always, it must be done in the spirit of restoration.

Recognize that our hearts and minds can lie to us. Your feelings are not always an honest representation of a situation. This does not discount your feelings or dismiss them. You feel what you feel, but your feelings may be lying. Think of times when you have convinced yourself that someone is mad at you, only to realize later they were just sick and reacted differently than they normally would. Or when we tell ourselves we are not good enough, or worthy, of having someone love us. There are countless examples of how we can lie to ourselves, we just need to be aware of this reality. We do not have to let our feelings dictate our reactions to any given situation.

Do your best to present yourself to God as one approved, a worker who has no need to be ashamed, rightly handling the word of truth (2 Timothy 2:15, Paraphrased). Study God's word and ask his Spirit to give you understanding. This is the first step in overcoming the lies we tell ourselves. Filter all of your intrusive thoughts through the verses you have studied. This does not mean you have to become a biblical scholar, but you may end up learning more than you intended to when you work at knowing God and knowing his word.

Chapter Six: Rehab

Be honest with yourself about your heart's condition. Allow yourself the freedom to review your actions and compare them to Jesus. After all, he gave us the example we ought to follow. Recognize the times when they do not line up. This is far easier to say than it is to do. I know this from experience. It took me many years of thinking I was on the right path, to realize I wasn't even on a path! I was lost in my own little world of self. It took me a decade to realize I had become exactly what I hated in the church. I was just self-righteous in the opposite direction.

Read the bible, not to prove your beliefs are right, but to find out what you need to change about your beliefs. God's word is living and active. This does not make it elusive to those who are seeking to understand it. Instead, it makes the verses come alive to you as the Spirit gives you the understanding. Read the Bible in translations you do not typically use. The different wording can often bring clarity to a verse that has not made a lot of sense.

Finally, surrender. Leave off your own agenda and submit to God's. After all, you are a worker in his kingdom, not the other way around. When you do this you will realize your own selfishness. For me, I recognized I was just like the rich young ruler—definitely not because I am so rich, but because I had things in my life I really did not want to give up in order to follow God.

Chapter Seven: The Realization

Read every verse you can find on the things you are afraid of. Look at how your fears affect your actions, verbiage, and body language. God knows what you are anxious about and has given us everything we need for life and Godliness (2 Peter 1:3). Know that your goal does not have to be to conquer your fears. Your goal should be to rely on God to be your defender.

Read the story of David and Goliath in 1 Samuel 17. See how fearlessly David stood against the defiant enemy of God. Understand this is not an attempt to encourage you to stand strong against your fears, or your own personal 'giants.' You are not David in this story. You are the Israelite army who is paralyzed by fear. Jesus is the one who slays giants. We rely on his power and strength. Jesus is the one who conquers death, not us.

Find ways to rely on his strength daily. This can be in ways we know we are weak. Maybe you have an addiction, struggle with anger, or you are just too busy to care about others. These are all ways you can place yourself in God's hands and allow his strength to shine through your weakness.

Chapter Eight: The Struggle

Look up every verse you can find on God's will. He absolutely will reveal it to you. Allow your mind to be changed. If you find yourself being stubborn on a certain topic, lay it before God! God has changed my mind repeatedly as I sought to grow closer to him. Remember to offer grace to people who have not allowed God to change their minds. Pray that those acts of grace might be a catalyst to help others finally submit to God's transforming power.

Instead of sitting down and waiting for God to show you some master plan, do the things you know he wants you to do. You know he wants you to love your neighbor. Are you doing that? You know he wants you to treat others in the way you want to be treated. Are you doing that? If you are not doing the small things you know God wants you to do, why do you think he will give you some great task?

Read Jesus' parable of the talents from Matthew 25:14-30. Now read it again. Look for the ways it parallels what the master is asking of his servants. Remember, we are servants in God's kingdom. Recognize that God will only give more responsibility to those who are already demonstrating responsibility.

You do not have to start an orphanage to serve God, just care for one fatherless child. You do not have to start a homeless shelter, a clothing pantry, a foreign mission, or non-profit organization. If you are not willing to show love and care for the one, why would you attempt to do it for the thousands? Love your neighbor. Help someone in need. Care for the lost. Offer shelter, clothing, comfort. Be the hands and feet of Christ. If you are faithful with little, he may call you to more.

Chapter Nine: The Body

Find out what you are passionate about and what you are good at. Now find ways you can use your talent and passion to share the gospel message. If you don't know what you are passionate about, ask yourself what ministry you would start if someone gave you $100,000. If you could spend the rest of your life doing one thing, what would it be? Make a list of what you currently do that is not a self-indulgent activity. Now you have a place to start in evaluating your passions.

Think outside the box. The four walls of a church building should not limit your ministry. If you are passionate about horses, you probably don't want to bring your horses into the church auditorium. But you could offer to teach people about horses. Talk to schools, homeless shelters, veterans' organizations, or crisis pregnancy centers. See if they have any ideas of how you could incorporate your knowledge and interests to bring encouragement or excitement into someone else's life.

Talk to your Christian peers about what they are passionate about. Encourage them in their endeavors or meet up with someone who has similar interests. Think civically—community centers, after-school programs, school boards, community development organizations, as well as the organizations mentioned above. These are all great ways to benefit your community and live out your role within the body of Christ; and, of course, support others in their roles.

Not everyone is hospitable and not everyone is adventurous. But, when an adventurous person teams up with someone gifted in hospitality, they can come up with incredible living room game nights, mystery dinners, or back-yard olympics. Find ways to work with others who have strengths you lack, or offer your strong-suits to others who could use your input.

Remember, whatever you do, be humble enough to accept help and be gentle when offering criticism. It is easy to rush past the rest of the body and forget that you are dragging them behind in the dust. It is also easy to resist change and hold the entire body back if you do not feel comfortable with a particular action. You are part of a body that needs to work together.

Chapter Ten: Broken

One thing to keep in mind is that breaking ourselves is not the goal with this, but admitting and recognizing our brokenness in the presence of God. The focus is not to humiliate ourselves or anyone else for our broken state because we are all broken. Brokenness is humanness.

We must first admit to ourselves that we made a choice to stop reflecting God's image to those around us. This internal dialogue, for me, often sounds like this, "Oh no! What have I done!" or something very similar.

Most of the time it also includes, "I hope no one saw that!" Because if no one saw it, then I was in the clear, right? It is within our nature to not want to admit when we make poor choices. This is the reason most people remain in an unrepentant state. This does not allow us to admit we are broken and leads to self-righteous attitudes.

Another step in the process is certainly crying out to God. Look at how often we see King David calling out to him. I have bawled my eyes out before God for the stupid and self-absorbed choices I have made. It is not an attempt to make me feel better, but an attempt to make God feel better. When I leave the focus on myself, the focus never shifts back to God. It is not about me—it is about him.

Next, make the decision to act differently. Find someone who can hold you accountable. Reach out to a friend and tell them not only what you did, but why you did it. Allow them to see your humanity and brokenness. This releases you from the pressure of trying to keep your actions hidden, and allows you to begin healing (James 5:16).

Finally, listen to those closest to you. Even the simplest things can make a profound difference. On the most simplistic level, someone might tell you, "Your voice sounds harsh. You should go make a cup of tea." At that point the choice is yours—get offended and remain in your brokenness or take the advice and soothe your brokenness. Recognize the people who God has placed around you, who have your best interest in mind, and allow God to speak through them.

Chapter Eleven: Faithfulness

There are three areas I want to emphasize in this final chapter. As I outlined above, faithfulness is more than just mental assent or adherence to a set of rules. That being said, these three areas are a crucial part of what makes faithfulness possible in the Christian walk.

First: Worship. We know worship goes far beyond just singing. Everything we do should be to give him glory.

Colossians 3:17 (ESV), "And whatever you do, in word or deed, do everything in the name of the Lord Jesus, giving thanks to God the Father through him." It's not just "knowing" that he is watching, but doing whatever we do to show God how much we honor him.

Remaining faithful in just this one area will shift our paradigm from being self-centered to being God-centered. Try it! Commit to faithfully worship God through your actions and see if, within a day, you are less selfish in your decisions.

Second: Fellowship. Hebrews 10:25 is a classic verse I always heard as a command to not miss a Sunday church meeting. "Not forsaking the assembling of yourselves together as some of you are in the habit of doing..." So I was taught you had better be in church every Sunday!!

But let's look into the context of this verse and see what the author was driving at. Starting back in verse 23, "Let us hold tightly without wavering to the hope we affirm, for God can be trusted to keep his promise. Let us think of ways to motivate one another to acts of love and good works. And let us not neglect our meeting together, as some people do, but encourage one another, especially now that the day of his return is drawing near."

The author here was pointing out how much we need each other! Jesus told us, "...in this world we will face trouble." James 1:2 tells us we should consider it a joyful thing to face these troubles because it tests our faith and produces perseverance! But this is not something we are meant to handle on our own. The author of Hebrews tells us we need to get together with other Christians as often as we can and encourage them. We need each other! We need encouragement!

Third: Prayer. Samuel the prophet was addressing the Israelites when he said this, "I will certainly not sin against the LORD by ending my prayers for you." —1 Samuel 12:23 (NLT). He took prayer so seriously that he considered it a sin against God if he stopped praying for Israel. Colossians 4:2 tells us to devote ourselves to prayer!

Of course we all know the verse in 1 Thessalonians 5:17 (KJV), "Pray without ceasing." When you pray, you are not talking to the people who might happen to hear you. You are talking to God! It doesn't matter if you use the wrong words, or get someone's name wrong, or even if you don't give God all the details. Matthew 6:8 reminds us that God knows our requests before we even ask.

James 5:16 (NLT) tells us to, "Confess your sins to each other and pray for each other so that you may be healed. The earnest prayer of a righteous person has great power and produces wonderful results." Prayer in community is powerful. Unity in prayer is also powerful. Faithfulness in prayer is powerful. Acts 2 again tells us the early church was steadfast in prayer, and fellowship, and worship.

End Note

This is the encouragement Paul gave in 2 Timothy 4:7-8, (NLT),

> *"I have fought the good fight, I have*
> *finished the race, and I have*
> *remained faithful. And now the prize*
> *awaits me—the crown of*
> *righteousness, which the Lord, the*
> *righteous Judge, will give me on the*
> *day of his return. And the prize is not*
> *just for me but for all who eagerly*
> *look forward to his appearing."*

If we can do that, if we can remain faithful until the end, if we can continue the race and see it through to the end, I guarantee you one day we will hear the master say to us, "Well done, my good and faithful servant, enter into the joys of the Lord!"

www.ingramcontent.com/pod-product-compliance
Lightning Source LLC
Chambersburg PA
CBHW071528120626
46550CB00006B/2388